Early praise for BRAND DELUS[...]
By: Bill Leider

"I am honored that you asked me to review the book. I observed many of your life lessons shared with me over the past 26 years deeply imbedded from cover to cover. A wonderful reminder of how lucky I am to have had you as a mentor for most of my adult business (and personal life)."

Eric Openshaw, *Vice Chairman, Deloitte Consulting*

"BRAND DELUSIONS is a blueprint for a journey to personal and corporate success. Regardless of your academic discipline or organizational mission, Bill Leider presents the essence of who and what we are in an intellectually engaging and provocative style, leaving you eager to begin your own brand strengthening journey and wanting more of his sage advice!"

Erroll Southers, *Adjunct Professor, Sol Price School Of Public Policy, University of Southern California; Managing Director for Counter-Terrorism and Infrastructure Protection, TAL Global, a renowned international security consulting organization*

"Wow. It's much more than a good read. This book should be required reading for every college student in the country who contemplates entering the business world - in any capacity."

Dona Wright, *mother of a college student about to graduate*

"By using a deceptively simple day-in-the-life allegory of a CEO's struggle to unify his team, Bill Leider reveals the essential truth that everyone in an organization acts to build or to destroy a brand. As you read BRAND DELUSIONS you begin to understand the power of removing your team's misconceptions about their roles in building customer perceptions and growing your business. Use Bill's insight to energize and focus your organization."

Don Roland, *retired CEO, Vertis, Inc., one of the largest printers of insert advertising in the U.S.)*

Brand Delusions

Brand Delusions

Exploding the myths and helping you improve
your Brand – professionally and personally

BILL LEIDER

For Arlene, my constant source of love and inspiration

Contents

Introduction: xi

Preface: xiii

Current Reality

1: Intrusion   1

2: Sales Speaks Up   13

3: Manufacturing Makes Its Case   23

4: Finance Has A Different View   35

5: Lunching On Questions   47

6: New Product Development – Passion Unleashed   51

7: Awakenings   59

8: Information Technology – A Break From Tradition   61

9: Reflections And Assessments   71

10: Human Resources – Poise, Professionalism And Politics   75

11: Premature Elation   85

12: A Little Panic   89

The Retreat

13: Introduction To Awareness   93

14: Candor And Conflict   95

15: A Much Needed Breather   105

16: A Break And A Breakthrough   107

17: The Trials Of Transition   111

18: Conspiracy Dressed As Collaboration   119

19: Light Bulbs For Some   123

20: What Not To Do – Sometimes The Truth Hurts   133

21: Awakening Continues   141

22: The Death Dance Of Resistance   145

23: A Line In The Sand   151

24: Crossroads   155

25: The Courage Of Surrender   159

26: Holistic Awareness Begins   167

27: Confession   175

28: Preparation For Re-birth   181

29: Preparation For Re-birth – Part Two   189

30: Preparation For Re-birth – Part Three   195

31: Getting Focused   199

32: New Definition – New Culture   205

What Next

33: Debriefing–Sort Of   219

Epilogue: It Needn't End Here   233

Acknowledgements   235

About the Author   237

Introduction

I was a very young entrepreneur when I heard the following words come out of Bill Leider's mouth: *"Your Brand is a commonly held set of beliefs and expectations about what you deliver and how you deliver it."* That simple sentence changed more than just my understanding of corporate Brands, but of personal Brands as well. It began what has become a two-decade-long exploration of this powerful definition, and a relationship with Bill Leider that has spanned that same time.

Before I met Bill, I'd never given much thought to the idea of "Brand." In my mind, Brands were the manufactured images that marketing and advertising agencies created for their corporate clients. Branding and Brand building were actions taken on behalf of a company. Executives hired a creative team to dream up actions, ads, and logos for the company or product.

I gave even less thought to people as Brands. The only individuals I would have considered "Brands" were celebrities, like Elvis or Madonna, or politicians, whose images, I assumed, were "manufactured" in the same way corporate Brands were manufactured. I was wrong about both.

What I have learned from Bill in these last twenty years is now being shared with you, the reader of this book. I believe it has the ability to alter your relationship with the concept of a Brand on multiple levels. Without question, it will help you see, perhaps for the very first time, how Brand impacts every area of a business: from accounting to customer service, and from marketing to manufacturing. It's told as a story. The characters struggle with their own understanding of Brand. And as they learn, you will learn with them. You'll experience the holistic nature of Brand through their journey. You will begin to see that there are no insignificant people when it comes to shaping a Brand inside an organization.

It's a business book, yes, but it would be mistake to look at this with only your business eyes. If you pay attention, you'll learn how this definition can positively impact you as an individual. "Behavior is the truest form of communication," Bill shared with me once. "Our words either confirm or deny truth."

And so it is with Brand. Like our values, our Brand is not what we *say*; our Brand is what we *do*. It is not just *what* we deliver, but *how* we deliver it. There are no insignificant acts. There are no meaningless conversations. There are no throwaway relationships. Everything we do and say, both in a company and in our personal lives, contributes to our Brand.

Brand Delusions will open your eyes to a truth that will positively alter how you see your business and your life.

Jeff Turner

Jeff Turner is an entrepreneur and a seasoned business executive of more than twenty-five years. He is currently the president of Zeek Interactive (a web design and technology company) the founder and creative force behind Real Estate Shows (one of the leading virtual tour companies in the country) and serves on the board of directors of Professionals Realty Group USA. He is widely regarded as a leading thinker on how to effectively use Internet tools, and is a sought-after conference speaker on topics related to emerging technologies.

Preface

What is a Brand? Why is it so important to fully understand, embrace and employ what truly defines a Brand on a holistic level? For starters, if you don't, you could be driving your customers to your competitors, no matter how effective your traditional "Branding" activities may be. On a personal level, the contradiction between your self- perception and the way others see you could have you living your life in the misunderstood lane. Think fractured relationships, lost career opportunities, more stress, and a host of other dysfunctions.

Most of us mistakenly think of a Brand as the identity of a product, a company or in some cases, a person. We see it as a name, visual images, and logos. We have some knowledge about what the product, or company, or person does. Typically, the strength of a Brand is seen as being synonymous with the number of people who recognize it, although some people also include a Brand's reputation when defining its strength.

That definition, for the most part, is only the identity piece, but it's as far as most people in business go in thinking about what constitutes a Brand. There are understandable reasons why conventional thinking has stopped at that place, at least at a conscious level. For starters, it neatly places control, responsibility, and accountability for Brands and Branding in the hands of the marketing and sales folks. Billions of dollars in marketing, advertising, media exposure, public relations, graphic design, product placement, social media, and more have been poured into "Branding"—the marketing and advertising world widely use the word *Branding* to describe a plethora of revenue-generating activities aimed at increasing awareness. Branding as we have come to define it is a concept brought to life through impressions and messages and images—all designed to build awareness. That's not necessarily a bad thing. But it's only part of a Brand. It just doesn't go far enough in understanding what a Brand truly is on a more organic level.

A major misconception about Brands is that name recognition is synonymous with strength. Not so. Name recognition is not a measure of strength; it's a measure of awareness. Strength derives from our experiences of and with a Brand. The experiences that consumers equate to a Brand's strength are conscious and unconscious, obvious and subtle, related and unrelated to product performance. Experiences can be inanimate (physically using the product with no other human interaction) and interpersonal (interacting with various people in the course of our use of a product).

The most important thing we must absorb to fully understand what defines a Brand is that a Brand is both messages (to develop awareness) and experiences (to develop strength). Messages describe us. They can create a particular mental image. Actions and experiences define us. Those experiences are what create substance. Brand messages contain promises. Promises beget expectations. Expectations become the criteria used to judge Brand performance. But promises and expectations are good only if they're kept and met. Otherwise they can bite the source that created them. And since customers feel the strength of Brands through their experiences, the full range of experiences you deliver places not just your Brand, but the heart and soul of your entire organization on display for all the world to see.

What we must further embrace is that Brand experiences encompass every conceivable encounter a person can have in their interactions with a company, its people, and its products. On an unconscious level, customers understand this. They do not sort their experiences into Brand and non-Brand categories. Everything experiential goes into one storage area or box in our brains, the Brand Box.

A shipping clerk who puts a dent in a box and ships it anyway bruises your Brand. A receptionist who is gruff on the telephone hurts your Brand. A credit manager who is too indifferent to work out a payment program with a long-time customer having temporary cash-flow problems diminishes your Brand. A "factory trained" service technician who shows up an hour late for an appointment with bad breath and a dirty uniform featuring a visible butt crack can become the unwitting star in a viral, Brand-sinking, laugh-riot, YouTube video. The Internet and other social media take the reach and speed of audience engagement to levels unimaginable just a few years ago. And it's well to remember that bad news typically creates an audience three times larger than good news does.

What I am saying, and what this book is about, is that when it comes to Brand strength, *everyone in the organization, in every functional area, at every level, performing every job, is a Brand ambassador. They hold that title of ambassador whether they know it or not, whether they agree with it or not, and whether they want it or not.*

There is significant danger in not seeing and acting on this fuller, more holistic definition of a Brand. It is simply this: if you are aggressively and effectively creating name awareness through your traditional Branding programs while not making the experiential elements (the strength part) of your Brand intrinsic in your focus, you could unwittingly be spending your Branding dollars to tell customers and prospective customers *not* to buy your products.

In today's world, it is not enough that customer-service people see the need to provide great customer service but do not see themselves as part of your Brand. Or that manufacturing people understand quality but see it outside the realm of your Brand. That is true for every person doing every job in your organization. A shipping clerk must see him/herself as a Brand ambassador. So must a billing clerk, a production worker, and a staff accountant. That, of course, means that every manager and executive in the organization must see him/herself in that ambassador role while simultaneously being subject matter experts and effective leaders in their respective areas of responsibility.

To fully embrace this reality three things are required:

- First, we must create a new definition of what constitutes a Brand;
- Second, you must create a culture that embraces that definition, lives it in letter and spirit; and
- Third, you must make certain that your core values are and remain aligned with this new reality.

Here is the new definition of a Brand. **Your Brand is a widely held set of beliefs and expectations about what you deliver and how you deliver it, validated by customers' experiences.**

This definition embraces and engages your entire organization. When executed effectively, it separates the winners from the rest of the pack. It affects everyone you touch and how you touch them, by all the people who touch them, no matter in what context. It goes beyond media message; it encompasses your customers' full experience of your product or service. For it is those experiences of the "what" and the "how" that create the truths that establish the real strength of your Brand in the hearts, minds and wallets of the people who matter most, your customers.

When you fail to see your Brand holistically, you create unseen dysfunction in your organization that, over time, becomes your cultural norm, a norm that limits your capabilities, lowers your aspirations, and makes true excellence unattainable.

How does one go about creating the culture I've just described? How do leaders make everyone Brand ambassadors while not losing perspective and having their people become confused, suddenly thinking that they all work for the sales and marketing arm of your company?

To help you understand and feel those experiential elements of your Brand, and to begin the process of adapting your culture to this new reality, I'm going to tell you a story that uses the definition of a Brand set forth above as its foundation. It's a story about a company and its leaders going through a cultural and strategic transition in defining their Brand and in learning how to embrace and execute the full spectrum of that Brand; in other words, learning to understand and define *what they deliver and how they deliver it,* and molding their culture to make that an executable reality. It is a coming-of-age story for the company and its executives as real people experiencing their deepest fears and feelings. The story illustrates the intellectual and emotional challenges facing virtually everyone in today's world. It's played out across the many areas of an organization's functions, activities, behavior and focus. It examines everything from strategy, to structure, to teamwork, to communication, to transparency, and all within the context of aligning with the company's core values; those lived as opposed to those merely talked about; because a Brand can only be sustained if the "what" and the "how" of it are consistent with the organization's core values.

The story, the company and the characters portrayed are fiction. They are, however, composites of real companies and real people drawn from hundreds of companies and thousands of people with whom I have worked and interacted over several decades. So is it really fiction?

I think you will find elements of yourself, your colleagues and your circumstances in this story.

I know that while the generic elements of a Brand may be universal, specific actions taken to build a Brand must be tailored to the uniqueness of each given situation, the style, culture and values of each individual company, and the personalities, strengths and weaknesses of its leaders.

With that in mind, I believe you will find abundant universal truths in this story to help you discover fresh, practical insights that you can adapt to your unique circumstances.

Enjoy your journey.

Current Reality

Chapter 1

Intrusion

Joseph Fenington never took afternoon naps. He didn't think it was right for a CEO. But today was different. Joe had been awake most of the night. For the first time in his company's history, they had to issue a product recall. A structural defect was discovered that could cause their blender to inexplicably crack. All the logistics of the recall had been worked out. The needed product fixes were in place, costs had been calculated, and revised forecasts and budgets had been prepared. What had kept Joe and his senior executive team up late was working out the final communication approach they would use with end users, dealers, the financial community, and the general public.

They were not of one mind about whether or not to tell the entire truth and to what extent they would accept responsibility. They all agreed on one thing: they had to protect their Brand. The spin doctors had their views. Joe had his. Joe finally prevailed, but he felt as if he'd been dragged through a swamp. His sense of integrity was coated with a layer of slime. Why did he have to defend telling the truth? To his own people! People he thought all shared the same values. To Joe, the discussion went deeper than the product recall. Telling the truth. Integrity. Those were two of the company's core values. Yet they'd fought a duel over living them. Joe was drained. At three in the afternoon, fatigue overpowered him. He staggered to his couch. Sleep came instantly.

A warm, inviting presence enveloped him like a blanket on a cold night. He stirred, opened his eyes, and saw a man was sitting in his private reading chair in the corner; it was an early Eames original that only Joe was allowed to use. The man didn't speak, and neither did Joe. He just stared at the man—and saw himself in twenty years: same build, plus maybe fifteen pounds; same square jaw; same sincere gaze; and a full head of salt and pepper hair, heavy on the salt.

"Who the hell are you, and how did you get in here?" said Joe.

"Do you always take afternoon naps? Guys your age usually have more energy than that," the man shot back.

"Do I know you?" asked Joe. He knew the answer. He was trying to be polite. He could not explain his inner calm in the midst of this eerie intrusion. Strangers didn't walk into his office without an appointment. Yet here he was. "What are you selling?" Joe asked, marveling at his own composure. At the same time his mind said, *"Just pick up the phone and call Security. Intruder gone; case closed."* But his gut said, *"Don't do that."* Joe listened to his gut.

"You're asking the wrong questions. You should be asking me how soon I can get started helping you," the man replied.

"I didn't know I needed your help," said Joe. "Hell, I don't even know you. I'm amazed that I haven't had you thrown out."

The man smiled, his first sign of emotion. "OK, I guess it's time to get down to business," he said. "Relax, Joe. Can I call you Joe?"

"I guess so. You don't seem to respect any other convention. And, by the way, I didn't get your name."

"How strong is your Brand?" asked the man.

"What? What do mean, how strong is my Brand? What kind of question is that?"

"A simple question. How strong is your Brand? Oh, and by the way, I'm not selling anything. Fact is, I'm here to help you secure your future."

Joe laughed. "Secure my future? If you knew anything about our company, you'd know that our future looks pretty secure without you." As he said the words, Joe felt a twinge in his stomach. A tiny lump of doubt pushed its way up through layers of confidence. Joe shoved it down. Like he always did.

They both fell silent. It felt like the rest between rounds in a fight. Breathe. Regroup. Focus.

Joe's mind began to play the tapes of his company's history. They had started modestly fifteen years ago, Joe and his two minority shareholders: Manny Factura, who ran production; and Desi Concepcion, their head of product design. With their life savings, loans from some family members, and a small line of credit from a bank (using their houses and every other earthly possession they owned as collateral), they embarked on their great American dream. Kitchen Sculpture was born. Their Vision was to captivate and capture the high-end market for small household appliances. They designed elegant products. They offered custom colors and finishes. Art and technology fused and gave birth to products equally at home in a kitchen or an art gallery. They were among the first to employ "smart" chips. They made products with brains. Toasters could sense when a piece of toast was about to burn and take corrective action. Irons knew when a delicate fabric was in danger of being singed and yelled a warning—in six languages. Blenders could whip up the best smoothies and puree the best baby food. Their products sold at high prices to people who cared more about status than cost. Many of their early customers bragged that their toaster cost more than their television.

Their planning was sound, their research was reliable, and their instincts were accurate. All that, combined with dedicated people, hard work, and a cooperative economy put Kitchen Sculpture solidly on the path to fulfill their dream. Although their niche was narrow, their dominance became overwhelming, and their profit margins were delicious.

They didn't rest on their laurels. As the cost of technology came down and their designs became widely known (even if not widely owned), competitors sprang up offering lower-priced knockoffs. Joe and his key executives crafted an aggressive strategy to enter the mid-price market. "If anyone is going to knock us off," Joe proclaimed, "it should be us."

Over the previous two years, they had acquired three companies to give them expanded production capacity and a solid presence in the mid-price retail sales channel. It seemed to be working—up to a point. The people in the acquired companies didn't think or act like Kitchen Sculpture people. They didn't all share the same values.

Communication was challenging, even over mundane things. Directives were frequently misinterpreted, sometimes with costly results. Misunderstandings fostered mistrust. Still, Joe's investment advisors offered encouragement. That's the nature of growth by acquisition, they said. A little patience and things will sort themselves out.

Joe had no experience in that arena. And sales were growing. But margins went from delicious to barely digestible.

More reassurance. Don't worry, Joe. That's to be expected. They'll get better over time as their presence becomes stronger. Volume increases will absorb more fixed costs. Just keep doing what you're doing.

To help strengthen expansion, Joe focused heavily on building their Brand. Even though theirs was not a huge company, Joe brought in a top ad agency with great Brand management credentials. They spent generously on image, positioning, and building consumer awareness in their mid-price channel. That strategy seemed to be getting some, but not all, of the results Joe wanted. While name recognition was up, it didn't generate the sales stampede they were expecting. Advertising and Brand management expenses were becoming a bigger percentage of sales.

Not to worry, his advisors had told him. That's to be expected in the early stages. We're fine, just where we want to be.

Joe's mind snapped back to the present. Now, he thought, this mystery man appears from God-knows-where, and the first thing he asks is, how strong is your Brand?

The man's voice ended Joe's reverie.

"Let me tell you why I'm here. Then let's get to work."

Joe was agog. "Look, if you think I'm going to hire you just because you barge in here and—"

"Stop," said the man. "I don't have time to waste. I told you, I'm here to secure your future. Don't play denial games with me. You need help with your Brand. If you don't know that, you're in worse shape than I thought."

The man continued as if Joe's cooperation was a given.

"I came back here from the great Brand Revolt of 2030. Oh, I know, that's still years off. But if you're lucky, you'll be around to experience it. Actually, the groundwork for the revolt started in 2015. Took fifteen years for enough people to get mad enough to create a full-blown revolution. Technology had to overpower apathy. When computer prices and smart-phone prices came down enough and speed, reliability, and ease of use increased enough, we finally had computers and mobile devices in almost every household. From then on, connecting through social media platforms became the order of the day across virtually all demographic categories. It was easy for people to talk about how fed up they were and what they could do about it. People like you, mesmerized by tradition, never saw it coming. Of course, I'm no one to talk. It got me too. I guess that's what makes me an authority."

Joe sat still as a rock, mesmerized. The man went on.

"By 2025 there was such a proliferation of Branding messages, it was hard for people to keep anything straight and remember who claimed what, whose promises meant something, and who was just full of crap. Web-based clubs sprang up all over the place, like *Consumer Reports* in real time. People shared their experiences and kept tabs on who was keeping their Brand promises and who wasn't. Finally, a massive revolt was organized—all done on the Internet, a revolution symphony in one movement. One day, all the Hollow Promise companies saw their sales dive to life-ending depths. No warning. No customers. Devastating. Brilliant. The justice of free enterprise was delivered by the unwashed masses and their collective power. It was the 'I'm mad as hell and I'm not gonna take it anymore' scene from *Network*. You should have seen the panic at those companies. Executives running around screaming, 'Are we at war?' God, it gives me goose bumps thinking about it."

Joe came out of his mute state. "Wait a minute. Are you telling me you came here from the year 2030 with a story about the collapse of maybe hundreds of companies? Because of what a lot of people thought was false advertising? Hah! You've got to be the biggest scam artist since Bernie Madoff."

Joe reached for the phone. He'd heard enough.

"It was eight hundred and sixteen companies, to be exact," said the man. "And how can you call me a scam artist? I'm not asking for anything! I'm not trying to sell you anything. I came here to save your ass."

Joe put the phone down.

"A little while ago, you asked me how I got in here. Now call your assistant, not Security," the man said, smiling. "She was at her desk when

I walked in. It was 3:05. Ask her if she saw me walk past her, open your office door, and go in. She'll tell you that no one approached your office, and no one came in. She'll get a little righteous and tell you she would never allow that to happen. Then she'll ask if you're all right, and if you want some aspirin. Go ahead, ask her, because you're starting to get on my nerves. I know we just met. I know you have no reason to believe me. But I also know your gut is saying that everything I'm telling you is true. Joe, trust your gut."

Joe picked up the phone and buzzed his assistant.

One ring and Alice's perfect, straight-from-central-casting voice chimed, "Yes, Mr. Fenington?"

"Alice, did a man come in at around three o'clock this afternoon and go into my office?"

"No sir, I would never let that happen. And I haven't left my desk since two thirty. I hope you don't think that I—"

"No, of course not, Alice," said Joe.

"Mr. Fenington, are you all right? Can I bring you some aspirin?"

Joe went numb for just an instant. "Everything's just fine, Alice. Didn't mean to disturb you. I know you're working on the Dumbarton Emporia project."

He hung up before Alice could respond. Joe stared at the man, awestruck.

The man smiled gently. "Good; now maybe we can move forward," he said.

"Wait a minute," said Joe.

"Now what?" said the man.

"You just described a financial meltdown. Our economy must have gone into a tailspin. The stock market would have crashed."

"Not at all. What happened following the sales nosedive at those Broken Promise companies was orderly. The worst offenders were forced to sell their companies to more responsible competitors at ridiculously low prices. Served the bastards right. Of course, the Consumers' Clubs dictated which companies would be sold and to whom. The companies that the consumers felt had made honest mistakes were given some time—not too much, mind you—to correct their mistakes and deliver on their Brand promises. The economy never skipped a beat. Shareholders came out just fine in the long run because better management teams now ran their investments. Almost every company in the country got the message, not just the eight hundred and sixteen: deliver on your Brand promises—or else!

"Technology advances gave companies a treasure trove of demographic and psychographic information. It helped them understand their customers, design better products, and subliminally influence their customers' buying decisions. Hell, they knew more about their customers than their customers knew about themselves.

"But here's the twist they never thought about. The same technology that put all that knowledge in the hands of companies also allowed customers to gather and share information. Information about all the companies that were selling all the goods and services that all the people in the country were buying. Not only could they gather and share, they could evaluate and act. In unison. A nation of consumers, millions of them, could exercise their might with the grace and precision of a synchronized swimming team. One day, without notice, power just shifted. The customers controlled the free enterprise system. Amazing. Companies that kept their Brand promises reaped rewards. Those that didn't were absorbed by those that did—and their managements suffered pain and trauma. Everyone else came out ahead."

Joe reflected for several minutes. The man sat, motionless. Finally, Joe spoke. "What about you? A few minutes ago you said that you didn't see it coming either. It got you too. What did you mean?"

"Well," said the man, "I was one of those CEOs who got to experience the pain and trauma."

"What did you do?" said Joe.

"First, I became incensed," the man replied. "I blamed everyone and everything except myself. I refused to take responsibility for my part, which, of course, was only about eighty percent." He chuckled as he said it. "Cleopatra may have been the queen of denial, but I was certainly the crown prince. When I realized there was no way to undo the harm, I succumbed to the stress. I had a sudden, fatal heart attack. No previous signs of illness," said the man. "I was standing in our conference room watching a news conference on TV. The head of one of the Consumers' Clubs was talking about my company as an example of not keeping your Brand promises. I guess you could say I took it too personally. God, what a mess. Although I probably made a bigger impact by keeling over in our conference room than I did while I was running, or should I say ruining, my company. Which is what brings me here."

"I don't understand," said Joe. "What does your untimely end in 2030 have to do with you being here today?"

"Well, the Big Guy and I are discussing my entry into that great country club in the sky, where everyone shoots three under par with no mulligans. I'm being given a second chance to help someone get it right. Think of it as heavenly community service. He sent me here to help a company with great potential that's headed down the wrong track. That would be yours, Joe."

"I don't get it. I mean, even if I believe your whack job story, why me? Why our company? We've got a great Brand. We're growing. We're expanding our markets. We should be a model for a 2030 survivor."

The man waited to let Joe finish bragging and defending. Then he spoke. "Listen, the Big Guy told me you were intelligent, you had potential, and you would listen. I hope he's right, because I don't see it. You're ignoring all the signs in your management reports. Your instincts are screaming, and you tell them to shut up. And don't think I didn't hear the doubt in your voice when you told me what a secure future you have. Joe, some day you'll learn that being dead makes you smarter.

"Look," the man continued, "I don't expect you to believe me. It's too crazy. Just do this. Operate on the possibility that it *might* be true. By the time we're done, I think you'll come around."

Joe pursed his lips, took a deep breath, and exhaled. "OK," he said. "I surrender. At least for now. What do you have in mind? How are you going to help me?"

"We're going to start by going through your company and finding out what your key people believe is your Brand," said the man. "How they define it. Then we're going to ask them what they think their role is in building it and strengthening it. I call it an internal Brand Assessment."

"Easy enough," said Joe. "We'll just head over to our marketing department and—"

"Whoa," said the man. "It's fine to start there. But to be clear, when I said 'your company,' I meant your entire company, every functional area. But we can start with marketing. What better place to begin than in the manger of misconception?"

"Wait; I still don't know your name. And how do I introduce you to our people?"

"The name's Brandon. Brandon Strong. You can introduce me as a special consultant; someone 'highly' recommended to help strengthen your Brand. By the way, who do you intend to include in our process?"

"I want you to meet the heads of Marketing, Manufacturing, Finance, Product Design and Development, Information Technology, and Human Resources."

"You're not including anyone from your newly acquired companies. Why not?"

"Well, you've just identified one of our issues. We acquired those companies because they were making inroads into the mid-price market for our kinds of products. They were doing it by knocking off versions of our designs that could be made for a lot less money because of some aesthetic design changes together with the elimination of our more-sophisticated performance features. In our eagerness to get into that segment of the market, we didn't do enough to examine the acquired companies' cultures and understand just how different we are. Those companies are driven by price, not quality. They're making our marketing, manufacturing, and design team crazy, not to mention me. We're trying to sort things out and integrate their people and ours. But for now, we're running those companies as subsidiaries, and they're not represented in our senior management structure."

"I think you'll find that the process we're about to begin can help you in that area," said Brandon.

"That would be a nice bonus."

As they walked down the hall toward the Marketing Vice President's office, Joe thought, *"This is, without a doubt, the craziest thing I've ever done in my career, but my gut says do it. So I'm going to keep an open mind. Maybe I can learn a little."* He had no idea what he was about to experience.

Chapter 2
Sales Speaks Up

Mark Selisman was waiting for them in his office when Joe and Brandon arrived. He looked prepared, just waiting for his audience to appear. He was poised but not relaxed. Joe sensed it and chalked it up to nerves. Brandon knew better. Mark sensed danger the way a gazelle senses a lion.

Mark made a great first impression on most people. He had that stereotypical All-American look: six feet tall, one hundred eighty five pounds; genetically well built, enhanced by regular workouts; dark blond hair with some gray creeping in; clean-cut, youthful face, baby crow's feet visible only during smiles; piercing blue eyes; broad, slightly crooked nose from his college football days. All in all, almost handsome, with a deep, resonant voice. Mark was about the same age as Joe: mid forties. High energy, ready smile. Nice package. If you looked deeper, you'd see that the smile was just south of genuine, and the friendly manner was superficial. Most people didn't notice. Mark's wardrobe completed the cool marketing-exec image. He was right out of a Ralph Lauren ad for *GQ*: dark blue suit; slate gray shirt; neon yellow tie, perfectly knotted.

Four thirty in the afternoon and every hair in place, with not a wrinkle in his clothes.

For all his camouflaged superficiality, Mark had done an outstanding job at Kitchen Sculpture. Customers loved him. He was accessible, patient, and a good listener. With Mark's leadership, the sales and marketing team always went the extra mile to take care of customers' needs and make them feel important. Mark and his team had developed and executed many innovative dealer programs that resulted in outstanding sales growth for both the dealers and Kitchen Sculpture.

But when it came to dealing with people inside of Kitchen Sculpture, other than Joe, and despite his degree in marketing with a minor in psychology from a prestigious Ivy League school, Mark had a Jekyll and Hyde personality. He was short-tempered, overly demanding, and dismissive of anyone who disagreed with him. People inside the company often saw Mark as arrogant and condescending.

Brandon understood both sides of Mark's behavior. He had seen it many times before. He knew that Mark posed a special challenge. *"This is going to be fun,"* he mused.

"Hi, boss," said Mark, smiling as they walked into his office. "To what do I owe the pleasure?"

"Good diction, nice inflection, warmly conveyed," thought Brandon. "Is it real or is it Toastmasters?"

Mark looked at Brandon, trying to read him, size him up. Friend or foe? Brandon's face was a stone mask, neutral and impossible to decipher.

Joe spoke. "Mark, I'd like you to meet Brandon Strong. Brandon is a consultant I've brought in to assess our Brand. He comes highly recommended. I know you're going to enjoy working with him."

"Of course I will," said Mark, reaching out to shake Brandon's hand with an I'm-going-to-break-your-fingers grip. *How predictable*, thought

Brandon as he squeezed back, partly in defense, but mostly to complete the Type A ritual greeting ceremony.

"So, what are we doing?" said Mark. "I didn't realize we needed help with our Brand. What have I missed, boss?"

Brandon spoke before Joe could respond. "Mark, how would you define your Brand?"

Mark stared blankly at Brandon while his wheels turned frantically: *Was this some kind of Brand 101 test? Did Brandon think he was an idiot? And why would Joe allow this? Had Joe lost confidence in him? Was this about their new mid-price product line? OK, it hadn't set the world on fire—yet, but he just needed a little more time and a slight boost in their ad budget. C'mon big guy, regroup. You can handle this. Piece of cake.*

Mark took a breath, smiled his I-know-the-answer smile, and said, "Our Brand is our public identity. It's what separates and differentiates us from our competitors. It's the story of our products' superiority, compressed into compelling messages that people remember. It presents our products in a way that makes people want to buy them. It's a picture; it's a promise; it's a perceived experience that we put in people's minds through the power of our advertising, marketing, and public-relations presence." Mark was on his game; he was just getting started.

Brandon cut him off. "Very good, Mark. Impressive answer."

Mark glanced at Joe out of the corner of his eye, looking for some sign of approval, or support. He thought he saw it, but wasn't sure.

Joe played silent spectator to the exchange. He agreed with Mark's answer. Normally, he would have expressed his agreement. Instead, he kept quiet. He could learn more that way. *How would Brandon see it,* he wondered?

Brandon stared intently at Mark. He spoke slowly and deliberately. "Mark, you've just given me the conventional definition of a Brand. I could go to any ad agency or Branding consultant in the country and get the same answer. Problem is, you've defined only a portion of your Brand."

Mark started to interrupt. Brandon froze him with a raised hand and a look. He went on. "I want to give you a definition of your Brand. But I don't want to discuss it now. I'd like you to think about it and its implications over the next few days. Then we'll talk."

"Your Brand is a widely held set of beliefs and expectations about *what you deliver and how you deliver it, validated by customers' experiences,*" said Brandon.

"I don't see that as being different from what I just described," said Mark. "No different, at all."

"I understand," said Brandon. "Take some time to think about it. All your work is about the message, making the promise, creating the expectation. That's part of the *what.* I want you to focus on the substance of the promise and the experience people have with your company. Not just with your products. Envision their entire experience of your company, throughout the customer life cycle. Go beyond the functions that you control—marketing and sales and customer service."

"You're asking me to think about things that are simply not my job," said Mark. Irritation was creeping in. Wheels turned again. *Who the hell does this guy think he is? Like, I don't have enough to do? Wait, Joe's not coming to my rescue. Step back. Assess. I've got to get Joe on my side. Be cool, big guy.* Mark loved his self-ordained nickname.

Mark flashed his warm you're-my-new-best-friend smile. "Of course I'll think about those things, Brandon," he replied. "But, I'm a little confused. I mean, how exactly should I be thinking about them? What the other people and the other functions in our company do, seems so straightforward. Our business is not rocket science. We design products, we engineer and manufacture products, we distribute them, we service them, we—"

"That's exactly what I want you to think about," said Brandon. "Give yourself an opportunity to trip over the obvious. Think about how all those things align with or detract from the experience of your Brand promise."

"I still don't see the connection, or the purpose," said Mark. *Gotta get Joe on my side of this exchange.* "If other people aren't doing their jobs, how or why does that change how we define our Brand?" *Why isn't Joe speaking up?*

"Mark, I don't want us to get ahead of ourselves," said Brandon. "Let me give you just one clue. Think holistically." Both Mark and Joe gave him glazed looks. Brandon continued. "Think of this organization as one connected organism. Everything is tied to everything else. And every single action, activity, task, idea, concept, strategy, thought—and every person—connects in some way to your Brand. Coming from that place, think about how this company *delivers* on the promises in your message. What kind of total experience do you deliver? I call that the *how* part of your Brand. We'll get out of your hair now," Brandon announced. "Thanks for your time."

"Wait," said Mark. "Joe, Brandon, do you want a written report or position paper? And by when?"

This time Joe spoke first. "Brandon is running this project, Mark. I'm a participant, just like you and everyone else."

"Everyone else?" Mark replied. "How many other people are involved? And, if we're talking about our Brand, why involve anyone beside us?" Wheels turning. *Danger. Control is slipping. I'm in charge of all Branding activity around here. What is Joe thinking, really? Need to play along. Gotta figure out Brandon's game plan. Stay cool, big guy.* He tried his best to be casual. "I mean, I'm just curious. It's a natural question, don't you think?"

Brandon took control. "Remember, Mark, I said think holistically. That means that everyone is involved. We're going to have a senior management retreat in a week or so. Organize your thoughts. Then, we'll talk again.

"I don't need a formal report. If you want to make some notes for yourself, that'd be a good idea. Does that work for you?"

"I know I'll be in town next week, so that should be fine." Mark was smiling again. *He hasn't told me specifically, but it sounds like all the VPs are involved. This guy knows how to play it close to the vest. Reminds me of me. No matter. Some of those guys will want a piece of me. Those bastards better remember who they're dealing with.*

A few more ritual pleasantries and Joe and Brandon headed back for Joe's office. Joe said, "That seemed to go reasonably well. What was your impression of Mark?"

"What did you think of my definition of Brand?" said Brandon.

"Interesting," Joe replied. "But I must tell you, I agree with everything Mark said. I still don't see what we have to learn here."

"You will. Soon. Just remember, think holistically. It will start to fall into place if you think holistically.

"Tomorrow, I'd like you to set up one-hour individual meetings with all your direct reports in their offices," said Brandon.

"No problem," said Joe. "Same agenda? And why in their offices? Why not mine?"

"Same agenda," Brandon replied. "It's more comfortable for them in their offices. Here's what I'd like you to look for in tomorrow's meetings. Notice how your people see themselves as supporting your Brand but not directly connected to it. Get how people see their roles as a bit distanced from the Brand messages emanating from Marketing."

"Who cares? What does it matter, as long as everyone is doing their job?" asked Joe.

"Subtle, unconscious, and profound," replied Brandon. "When the connection is linear and not holistic, people's energy, focus, and commitment are inconsistent. So are their results. The strength of your Brand suffers, usually in ways that you don't know about and can't measure. Even though people are working their buns off."

After a minute of pondering, Joe spoke. "So, you're telling me that when people's connection to our Brand is linear, like a chain, rather than being holistic and interconnected, that we experience lower productivity and lost sales? Is that what you're saying?"

"That's exactly it," said Brandon. "And you can add lost creativity, resourcefulness, and teamwork to the list."

"I'm sorry, I just don't see it. I think you're splitting hairs beyond the point of making any difference in the way people perform. If someone is doing his or her job, none of what you're saying will make any difference."

"Joe, do you have any performance incentives around here?"

"Of course we do," said Joe.

"Why? Why do you have them?"

"C'mon, Brandon, you know exactly why. I don't have to spell it out."

"OK. Think about the better results you get when you connect self-interest to corporate goals and reward the achievement of those goals. Then think about why people work so hard to achieve your company goals. Are they doing it for the company or for themselves?"

"I think some of both."

"Bullshit. Take away the performance incentives and watch how dramatically your results suffer. Oh, I know there's some degree of personal pride and self-worth attached. But it's not enough to achieve and sustain the performance you want."

Joe reflected before he spoke. "So you're telling me that people don't give a damn about the company, just about themselves?"

"Not exactly, and you know it. Look, all of us operate from a place of self-interest. It's basic to our survival. When you put performance incentives in place, you're marrying the self-interests of your employees with the interests of the company. When you celebrate goal achievements, you're rejoicing on behalf of the company—which, by the way, doesn't exactly hurt your net worth—and your employees are celebrating the extra bucks and the power that recognition brings. Power is another form of currency. When you design a really great incentive program, the line between personal goals and company goals gets so blurred that after a while it virtually disappears. There's complete harmony. When that happens, peoples' attitudes and behavior take on a holistic tone."

"Are you suggesting that we have to devise some kind of incentive program around our Brand?"

"Now don't start getting literal on me, here. You're way too smart for that."

"Just testing you," said Joe as he smiled. "But I think you are saying that there has to be something stronger and more compelling than just someone doing his or her job, even if it's done well, and achieve goals and earn bonuses and kudos."

"You got it. And tomorrow, in our meetings, try to listen with a holistic ear. See if you can sense what the connection is between people's beliefs about their jobs, and your Brand."

"I think I understand a bit better now," said Joe. "I still don't think I agree, but I can listen for what you're asking about."

"That's all you need to do right now."

Meanwhile, back in his office, as soon as Joe and Brandon left, Mark called in Sharon, his assistant. She'd been with him almost since he arrived at Kitchen Sculpture five years ago. He trusted her completely.

"Sharon," he said, "this is top secret. Use your private network. Find out everything you can about Brandon Strong. And I want to know every person Brandon talks to, what he says, what they say. Everything. Get back to me as soon as you learn anything. All verbal, nothing in writing, no e-mail. Understood?"

Sharon was curious. But she knew better than to ask. She'd learn in due time. "Understood," she answered. *Game on.*

Meanwhile, in Joe's office, as he and Brandon began to say good night, Brandon said, "Oh, about Mark. Very intelligent, well schooled, seems to be dedicated and hardworking. Now we'll find out about his passive-aggressive tendencies."

"What the hell are you talking about?" Joe asked. "Mark is all the things you said and more. He's creative, loyal, committed. He's done great things for this company, and I don't appreciate you saying—"

"Stop." Brandon held up his hand and smiled. "It's way too early for you to get defensive. Just let things unfold. You'll see what I mean, soon enough. And don't worry; whatever happens, it's all fixable. Good night, Joe."

Joe sat alone in his office, pondering the events of the last couple of hours and reflecting on Brandon's words. *Holistic? Linear? Subtle? Unconscious? Profound? Passive-aggressive behavior? Isn't he making things sound more complex than they are? Inventing problems and issues that don't exist? We've spent a small fortune designing performance incentives. We have good metrics in place. They work well. Our people seem motivated and results-driven. This is nonsense. Isn't it?* Up sprang his familiar stomach twinge. This time he didn't push it down. He had to admit, he was curious about what he might learn tomorrow. He'd soon find out he wasn't at all prepared.

Chapter 3
Manufacturing Makes Its Case

The first person on the meeting list was Manny Factura, Vice President of Manufacturing. Manny was one of Joe's minority shareholders. He'd been there from the beginning, when they hatched their vision at Joe's kitchen table.

In his early fifties, Manny had a long, broad face—oversized, really—with a flat nose that looked transplanted, hangdog cheeks, pointed chin, and deep-set brown liquid pools for eyes. In another life, he might have been a basset hound. Of medium height, with thinning, mostly gray hair, stocky and solid, he could look fifty or seventy, depending on his mood. Unlike Mark's *GQ* image, Manny's clothes looked like a blind man at the bargain rack in a thrift store had pulled them together. He was the butt of a lot of jokes by the best-dressed set around the company. Manny was unperturbed. He didn't see the importance of caring about what he wore. He saw the importance of people. All people. His genuineness was a blessing and a curse.

Manny instantly bonded with kindred spirits. Manipulative people, people who had hidden agendas, or people who were less than authentic usually misinterpreted Manny. They thought he was too naive, too trusting, or just plain stupid. Manny was none of those. Just because he had a trusting nature didn't mean he trusted everyone. He was street smart. He could smell a phony like a DEA dog could smell heroin. And like a dog, he held people like that at bay. He didn't change his nature. He just never let the phonies get too close to him.

Joe was the company's charismatic cheerleader. Manny was its rock of stability. He was the glue that held people together through the stormy times. If there was a crisis, it was Manny's lifeboat you wanted to be in.

His office was located on the mezzanine level, with a large window overlooking the plant. Furnishings were on a par with his wardrobe, an assemblage of odd pieces of furniture in various states of distress. Each piece was chosen for utility, or perhaps to save it from the scrap heap. Stacks of reports and files were everywhere, making the room one huge filing cabinet. But it worked the way Manny wanted it to work. He knew where everything was, and he could instantly access what he needed.

He spent as little time in his office as possible. He preferred to prowl the factory floor like a friendly bear, going up and down the aisles observing, talking to people, but never interrupting their work. He learned more that way than he ever did poring over the reams of data in his management reports. He got his college degree at night school. He got his education on the streets. He was whip-smart in both arenas. He just preferred to learn through human interaction.

He loved his people. He treated them as friends. They would rather have died than let him down. He never had to demand anything. He just had to ask.

He also loved his machines. He treated them the way a veterinarian would treat a puppy: lots of love and preventive medicine. If the machines could have licked him, they would have. Instead, they showed their gratitude by running smoothly and continuously.

"How're you doin'?" said Manny, his right hand extended. "I'm Manny, nice to meet you." He enveloped Brandon's hand in his own. His hands were large and calloused; his grip, firm and friendly. He didn't wait for an introduction.

"Manny, meet Brandon Strong," Joe said. "Brandon is a highly recommended consultant who's going to help us evaluate and strengthen our Brand. Brandon, meet Manny Factura, our Vice President of Manufacturing. Manny is responsible for all our manufacturing activities for all divisions, including our new acquisitions."

Manny responded, "Boy oh boy, suddenly I feel important. Hey Joe, how about that raise you and I've been talkin' about?" All three of them smiled.

Brandon knew from the moment he saw him that Manny was the genuine article. Not a phony bone in his body. No reason for small talk. He got right into it. "Nice to meet you, Manny," he said. "Let me cut right to the chase, if that's OK with you."

Manny smiled. "My kinda guy," he said, looking at Brandon and Joe. "What can I do for you?"

"Manny," Brandon began, "what's your definition of your Brand?"

Manny shifted his weight from right to left, some discomfort revealed in his body language. "I mean, no offense, Brandon, but shouldn't you ask Mark that question?" said Manny. "This sounds, like, out of my league, if you know what I mean."

"Just give it your best shot. This isn't a test. I'm not grading you. I'm just interested in how you see it."

"OK, here goes. Our Brand is all the stuff that the people in marketing say it is in all of our advertising. It's the great design of our products, their features and functionality, dependability, snob appeal. Oh excuse me, I meant to say uniqueness and sculptural essence, like our advertising guys constantly hammer into me. I mean, what the hell else is going to make people want to pay four hundred bucks for a damn toaster?" Manny was getting wound up. "It doesn't make women eternally young. It doesn't make men forever virile. It makes fuckin' toast, for chrissakes. That's our fuckin' Brand." He fell silent and took in a few slow, deep breaths. The veins in his neck that had popped out during his tirade receded, and the color in his face, deep red when he finished, returned to its normal swarthy tan.

Joe sat and listened in stunned, silent disbelief. As naive as it seemed, in fifteen years he had never heard Manny explode like that. Never heard Manny describe their Brand, their products with such scathing sarcasm heading toward rage. *What the hell was going on here?* Joe wondered.

"Manny, what's wrong? What the hell was that about?" Joe said. "We've been together for a long time, since the beginning. I've never heard you go off like that. Never. And we've had our moments."

"Listen, Joe, things are changing around here, and I don't think you get it, at least not all of it. I figured since you brought in Brandon, here, to work on our Brand, it's OK for me to say what's really on my mind. So I did. Besides, if it helps me get off my blood pressure medicine, that'll be my contribution to reducing our health insurance premiums." Manny smiled, trying to relax the room. It didn't work.

Now Joe was agitated. "What do you mean, I don't get it?" he snapped. "What exactly don't you think I get? And when the hell did you become an authority on our Brand? Or our product design?" Joe was headed for a street fight, fast.

Brandon stepped in. "Listen guys," he said, "calm down. This is an important issue, and there are obviously some raw nerves here. So let's just step back, take a deep breath, and try to be objective."

"Manny"—Brandon looked straight into those basset hound eyes— "please elaborate. Give us your take on the whole Brand thing and why it's pissing you off the way it is. Start to finish. And, Joe, just sit there and listen. Take it in. Don't react. Not yet, anyway. Fair enough?" Both men nodded, but Joe was still struggling to regain his composure.

Manny didn't hesitate. "It's all the condescension from Sales and Marketing. It's the impossible demands about deadlines for shows and special promotions with late notice and inadequate lead times. On top of that, we're expected to meet all our regular ship dates to our customers. And oh, by the way, no overtime and no hiring. Profit is declining. Just dump it all on Manny. He'll figure out how to make it happen. He always does. What am I, a fuckin' magician?" Manny was not about to get off his blood pressure medication any time soon.

"Let me tell you two something else," Manny went on. "Our problems go way beyond our flagship products. Some of our biggest problems are at our three new plants. Guys, the people over there live in a different world. And they don't see quality and service and customer satisfaction and a whole bunch of other things anywhere close to how we see 'em. Joe, you think that because they're part of Kitchen Sculpture and a bunch of people from our HR department did some orientation nonsense that they all of a sudden think and act like us? Well, you're wrong. They're not only not on the same page; they're not even in the same damn book."

Joe was visibly shaken. He knew Manny would never lie. How had he been so out of touch? He had to learn more. "Manny, give me some examples."

"What, you don't believe me?'"

"I do believe you. That's why I want some examples. I need to learn more, and I need to start right now."

Brandon stood back, observing the two men and thinking, *What a shame they don't talk like this more often. Something in the overall dynamic of this group is way off.*

"OK, you asked, you get. One of the new divisions is just starting to use Statistical Process Control in their manufacturing operations. All these years they thought they could inspect quality into their products, instead of making 'em right the first time. Their reject rates and machine down times don't meet our standards. That drives up costs, lowers our margins, and makes it harder to deliver on time. They're in the process of implementing the process, but I'm havin' trouble lighting a fire under their asses. They just don't have the sense of urgency I want from them."

"Why didn't we discover the quality issue during our due diligence before the acquisition?" Joe asked.

"We did," Manny said. "And we pointed it out. Our attorneys said it was a minor problem, and we could fix it quickly and inexpensively after we closed the deal. It was important to get the acquisition done quickly because the price was right, and we didn't want to give 'em a chance to shop our offer. Like our lawyers even know what SPC is, let alone how to implement it."

"Why wasn't I informed?" Joe asked, his tone more demanding than questioning.

"You were in Europe at the time, lookin' at strategic marketing alliances, if you recall," said Manny.

"Oh right, right," Joe said, stroking his chin as he recalled the situation. "Everyone I talked to said that, aside from a few minor glitches that we could fix after the close, everything was a go. I approved it over the phone. Shit. Why didn't I talk to you?"

"I'll drink to that," said Manny. "Look, I could go on for hours, but let me give you just one more for now, OK?"

Joe nodded.

"Some of the sales and marketing people in those divisions have some good insights about what our mid-price dealers and end users want in our products. But I don't think they get listened to at all. They tell me they've been told that it's their job to elevate the taste levels of the middle market and bring them up to our standards of elegance and quality. I never heard such shit in my life. I mean, I'm no marketing guy, but who doesn't listen to their customers?"

"Wait a minute," said Joe. "How and why are the marketing people talking to you?"

" 'Cause, according to them, I'm the only guy who'll listen to 'em. I mean, like every time I visit a facility, they're waiting to pounce on me and bend my ear. What the hell is goin' on between them and Golden Boy? I mean Mark."

"Oh, so this is about you and Mark," said Joe.

Brandon had to work hard to suppress the smirk that had crept into his face. He was not surprised that Manny and Mark had an oil-and-water relationship, but his concern was rising at its intensity. He was, however, impressed by Joe's willingness to face it head-on.

"Hey Joe, you wanna' travel life's little highway in the denial lane, or do you really wanna' know what's goin' on?" Manny replied, irritation crawling up his throat.

"OK, OK, sorry. This stuff is coming at me pretty fast. It's a big pill to swallow in one gulp."

"Well, at least we're finally talking. Hell, if enough of us get involved, we'll be able to start buyin' Rolaids at Costco. Look how much money we'll save." Manny snorted a laugh, trying to lighten the moment before he went on. "Hey guys, I apologize. I really went off on a tangent. I guess I needed to vent. You asked me about our Brand. None of the stuff I talked about has anything to do with our Brand."

Now Brandon jumped in. "Manny, Joe, everything you two talked about relates to your Brand."

"It does?" said Manny. "Then maybe I'm confused. Before I went off on my road-rage rant I gave you a definition of our Brand. How does anything I said relate to that?"

"Manny," Brandon said, "I'm going to give you my definition of Brand. *Your Brand is a widely held set of beliefs and expectations about what you deliver and how you deliver it, validated by customers' experiences.* I'd like you to think about it for a few minutes before you respond. You see, everything you two talked about had to do with the *how* part of that definition. Well, everything except the story about the sales staff at your division. That was part of the *what*. Manny talked about the potential for late deliveries, gross profit erosion, and the possibility of faulty product shipments. Manny, let me ask you this question. Don't all of those things impact your customers' total experience of your company?"

"Well, partly," Manny answered. "I mean, how does our gross profit decline affect our customers' experience? They don't know about it. It's not reflected in our products or service."

"Manny, if profits are reduced, can't that cut into next year's product-development budget? And if you have fewer resources for product development, can't that mean less innovation, or compromises in cutting-edge design? And can't that affect your customers' future experience of your products?"

"Hmm," Manny mused.

"Now, let me tweak my definition of your Brand," Brandon said. "Your Brand is a prevailing body of beliefs and expectations resulting from people's *total experience* of your company. You see, gentlemen, you deliver an experience far beyond your advertising message and your products."

"So," Manny replied, "you're sayin' that everything we do that impacts someone's belief about our company is part of our Brand?"

"Correct," said Brandon.

"I'm not sure I can buy that."

"Why not?" Brandon asked.

"Well, for starters, I don't think people think of a Brand that way. I don't think that if a product ships a little late, but it's a good product, people think there's something wrong with the Brand. Or, if occasionally, a company sells a defective product, that the Brand is bad."

"Really? Let me ask you a question or two. Suppose that a company did what you just said: occasionally shipped late and had a few defective products. They hired an ad agency to promote their Brand. The ad agency came up with an ad campaign and the message was: 'Buy our products. They're really great, except we sometimes ship late and some of them are defective.' What would you think? What would you do?"

"First thing I'd do is fire the ad agency."

"Why?" Brandon asked. "For promoting truth in advertising?"

"C'mon, Brandon, what kind of moron is gonna' send out that kind of advertising message? Nobody in his right mind would buy the product."

Brandon paused to let Manny's words bounce around his brain, and Joe's as well. "So what's the difference whether the message comes from the advertising department or from the people in manufacturing? It's the same message, isn't it?" asked Brandon. "Manny, do you think that the only messages about your Brand that count are the ones coming from your marketing people?"

Manny stared intently at Brandon, then at Joe. "Holy shit," he finally said. "It's so obvious. It's right in front of my nose. I never made the connection. I mean, we're all over quality and on-time shipments and standing behind defects and controlling costs and balancing inventory and never having stock-outs and all that good stuff. I just never saw it as our Brand."

"What do you see it as?" asked Brandon.

"I see it as good product quality and good product support."

"And if the purpose of good product quality and good product support is to give your customers the kind of experience you want them to have, and for them tell their friends and spread the word and buy more products, then why isn't that part of your Brand? What makes it different?"

After a long, thoughtful silence, Manny, nodding his head, said, "When you put it that way, I guess it is our Brand. There's no difference."

Joe nodded firmly, but chose to remain silent.

"There actually is a difference," said Brandon. "And that difference can be powerful. When you think about product quality, you're looking at what you control. When you think about your Brand, you're thinking beyond what you control to a customer's total experience. That complete experience is what creates the beliefs and expectations you want people to have about what they will receive when they do business with you."

"Good God," said Manny. "How and when did you come up with this stuff, Brandon?"

"That's a long story I'd rather not get into right now." Brandon smiled.

"Manny, I'd like you to think about what we discussed. Think about the implications for all of manufacturing if you shifted your beliefs and understanding about what your Brand really is. Think about how your people might see their jobs differently, about how they might act and perform differently. Think about how your coordination with other functional areas might change if everyone saw things through the lens of your Brand. And think about the results that you and everyone else might get that are different from what you're getting now."

"I will," said Manny. "Hey, Brandon, Joe, is it OK if I bring in some of my senior people and have a little round-table discussion?"

"Great idea," said Brandon. Joe nodded his agreement.

"We'll all get together in about a week at an offsite retreat, the whole management team, and continue this," said Brandon.

"Sounds good. Hey, guys," said Manny. "I really apologize for goin' off like I did."

"I'm glad you did," said Brandon. "If you hadn't, this discussion wouldn't have gone anywhere."

"Yeah, I guess you're right. Then thanks for letting me vent. I needed that. You know, I feel more relaxed now than I have in months."

Joe looked intently at Manny. "You know, one of our core values is about telling the truth. Why the hell did you keep all this bottled up for so long? You, of all people. Why didn't you come to me? You're the rock, Manny. You're the most stable leader in this whole damn company."

"Joe, I guess I just got so bogged down in the problem I couldn't see the forest for the trees. Besides, I know how highly you respect Mark. And I really do know how much he's done for our company. Just because I don't trust him, doesn't mean I'm right. Anyway, I guess I just didn't wanna' make waves. We've all been under a lot of pressure lately. I just sucked it up and tried to work it out silently. You know, I never even looked at the situation in terms of living our values. Bad move, huh, Joe?"

"Very bad. If I want the silent type, I'll go hire Marcel Marceau, OK? And, Manny, I refuse to be held responsible for your high blood pressure any more. Got it?"

"Got it," said Manny.

As Joe and Brandon headed over to Finance for their next meeting, Joe couldn't wait to start debriefing. Brandon stopped him.

"Joe, I know you want to talk about this right now. I'm asking you to hold off. Just take it all in and think about it for now. We'll have plenty of time to talk later. Don't jump to conclusions before you have a chance to get a more comprehensive view from more of your people."

Brandon stopped in his tracks and turned to face Joe. "Actually, Joe, there is one thing I would like you to think about," said Brandon.

"What's that?"

"You know, in Manny, you've got a very capable, committed, hard-working manufacturing executive, a true friend and a partner. He's been here from day one. And with all that, he sees his work and his responsibilities as related to your Brand, as supporting your Brand, but not an integral part of your Brand. How much more effective do you think the manufacturing area of your business would be if everyone in it saw themselves and their work as an integral part of your Brand? Don't say anything. Just think about it, Joe."

"Brandon, that's the same thing you asked Manny to think about."

"True," Brandon replied.

"Well, you're right. I need to ponder that one for a while. And I must say, you've produced some big surprises for me in just our first meeting. So I guess I need to play it your way. But you need to know that right now, I'm jumping out of my skin. What do you think we'll hear in our next meeting?"

"Let's go find out," said Brandon.

Chapter 4

Finance Has A Different View

The nameplate on the office door said Benjamin Counter, Vice President of Finance. When they entered, Ben's back was turned. He was staring at his computer screen on the workstation behind his desk. The contents of an Excel spreadsheet filled the screen as Ben's eyes laser-locked onto some data in the lower right-hand corner.

"Aha," he chortled, "I knew you'd be hiding there. Thought I couldn't find you, huh? I'm gonna nail the guy who thought he could bury you here and I'd never look. Let's just see what he has to say for himself, and if he still has a job when I'm finished with him."

Ben turned and smiled. "Hello, Joe. And hello, Mr. ..."

Brandon held out his hand. "Strong, Brandon Strong. Nice to meet you, Ben."

Joe jumped in. "Ben, I've engaged Brandon to help us strengthen our Brand. He's a renowned consultant and comes highly recommended. Brandon, as you know, Ben is our Vice President of Finance."

Ben's nickname was Bean. He didn't like it, but his job made it a natural. It didn't help matters that he shaved his head. And while shaved heads might be stylish, the shape of Ben's head wasn't. It was oblong.

The back of it protruded as if a brain too large for its container had pushed it out. Small, inquisitive brown eyes, framed by tortoiseshell glasses perched atop a long, straight nose. A thin, neatly trimmed moustache over even thinner lips completed the picture. Ben's head was a conversation topic in the office. He didn't seem to notice, and if he did, he didn't seem to mind. He had more important things to worry about.

Ben's purpose in life was to measure everything that existed in the world of business. His pace was quick and his mind quicker. For Ben, the color gray and words like *maybe* and *perhaps* did not exist. Things were either black or white. Answers were either yes or no. The existence of gray, in any form, was a sign of uncertainty, or indecision, or a lack of clarity. According to Ben, anyone who disagreed with the idea that everything could be measured was avoiding accountability, and that was a moral felony. Last year he developed an algorithm for determining the return on investment from participating in trade shows. Everyone said it couldn't be done. The Bean did it.

Ben was short and slight of build, with a small paunch. His wardrobe choices were more a statement of personal philosophy than fashion. No grays or muted colors. Everything was crisp and in stark, compatible contrast to one another. His shirts were the whitest white, his ties cherry red or neon blue or inky black. His suits were black or navy. Simple, crisp, decisive. When others in the company emulated Ben's dress style, they were labeled "Bean Boys." His only form of exercise was running around the office, carrying out his own personal mission—measure, analyze, and report. Ben drank enough coffee to justify having his own plantation. That seemed to be his only vice. Or perhaps it was a virtue, since Ben had more energy and capacity for work than any three people combined.

In his late forties, Ben had had an impressive Ivy League education. He spent several years working for one of the Big Four accounting firms before making the leap to private industry. He shaved his head when he left the rigid confines of public accounting. It was a kind of molting ritual by which Ben thought he could mystically shed his anal habits with a few razor strokes and expose the charismatic leader trapped inside. People who knew him before and after often commented, "What was he thinking?"

He had come to Kitchen Sculpture ten years ago. The original Chief Financial Officer didn't have the skills or sophistication needed to deal with the complex needs of a larger organization. Ben did. His inner charismatic leader, however, never emerged; his anal persona remained firmly rooted. But Ben's financial savvy, logical mind and analytical skills earned him the respect of his peers, subordinates, and, of course, Joe.

He quietly assumed the role of Exalted Devil's Advocate. When everyone fell in love with an idea and wanted to throw resources at it, Ben could often find a fatal flaw in the logic and show people why they were about to pour money down the sewer. He did it respectfully, always attacking the logic, never the person.

Except where Mark Selisman was concerned. The two of them constantly locked horns. It often got personal. Both insisted it wasn't. Everyone else knew better. They were playing a game of "Dad likes me better" when it came to winning Joe's approval. Joe tried his best to stay neutral, objective, and issue-focused. It didn't matter. For Ben and Mark, there was always an exuberant winner and a disgruntled loser. Ben's approach was to gather the information and analyze it till the little bits of data screamed for mercy. He always presented cogent, measurable arguments to support his position. Mark, on the other hand, often urged everyone to think outside the box, to go where no one had gone before, to not allow themselves to be imprisoned by outdated tradition and linear thinking. They were both forceful presenters. Experience showed that they were each right more than they were wrong. It made for lively meetings.

"I'm curious," said Brandon. "What got your juices flowing in that Excel analysis? Do you often talk to worksheets?"

"Oh, that," said Ben sheepishly. "Don't mind me. I just get carried away when people try to hide things from me and I find them. I don't know why people keep doing it. They know they can't get away with it. I think that they think it's some kind of game. Only I don't feel like playing." Turning to Joe, he said emphatically, "We're talking about real money here, Joe. It's what you and I were talking about last week. It's Division Two." He turned to Brandon to explain. "They produce our new mid-price blender line, Brandon. They've been misclassifying some advertising expenses on the Branding campaign for our new Dream-Blend line. The marketing people are trying to make themselves look better about early results in the campaign. This is the second month in a row I've caught them trying this kind of petty crap. Joe, unless you tell me otherwise, I'm about to go over there and give a few people some heartburn."

"Let's table this for the moment," said Joe. "I want us to focus on what Brandon is here to talk about."

"Oh, sure," said Ben. "Sorry for going off on a tangent, Brandon. I can get carried away when I find things like I just found. Right, Joe?" Joe smiled his agreement.

Brandon said, "Ben, I'd like to discuss your perceptions about your Brand."

"Sure."

"How would you define your Brand?" asked Brandon.

"Well, for starters, I don't go along with all the standard marketing mystique about what our Brand is. I get what the marketing people are saying about identity, image, recognition, and all that stuff, but I have a different take.

"I think our Brand is an asset. Its three main components are name recognition, name attractiveness, and name retention. Its purpose is to bring in revenue. Its cost is all the money we spend to create it and sustain it, even though it doesn't appear that way on our balance sheet. It appreciates in value when we hit the mark with our message and our campaigns and sales exceed our projections. It depreciates when we do things to tarnish it; or when we send messages that drive people away from us rather than toward us. It diminishes in value when our competitors send more compelling messages than ours, or when people get tired of our products and stop buying them, or when we don't maintain a consistent enough message for people to remember us. That's what I believe our Brand is."

While Brandon stood, slowly processing Ben's words, Ben reclined in his chair, sipped his coffee from a mug that always seemed full, and allowed a satisfied half smile to brighten his face. Joe, although he'd heard Ben expound on Brand before, was taken with the passion in Ben's presentation. It wasn't like him.

Brandon broke the silence. "Ben, that's a most interesting definition. I'm curious. How do you and all the people in finance, accounting, and administration fit within your definition? What part of the Brand do you comprise?"

"We're not part of it at all. Our job is to measure the relative value of our Brand at any given point and let everyone know where we stand— how we're doing with our Brand's performance."

"So, nothing your area does reflects, one way or the other, on your Brand. Is that what you're saying?"

"Precisely," said Ben.

"And therefore, nothing you do adds to or detracts from the value of your Brand. Is that also true?"

"Yes, yes, it is," replied Ben. Then he hesitated, and reflected. "Actually, we do add value," he said, "considering that our input about our Brand's status helps the people in marketing do their jobs better."

"Kind of like a scorekeeper at a baseball game?" Brandon asked.

"I guess you could put it that way."

"Let me give you another definition of your Brand," said Brandon. *"Your Brand is a widely held set of beliefs and expectations about what you deliver and how you deliver it, validated by customers' experiences."*

Ben sat quietly for a moment, sipping his coffee. He spoke slowly, weighing the significance of each word before he let it escape. "I understand. And I don't think that changes anything I said about my group's role in it."

"You know, Ben," said Brandon, "I hear you're big on accountability. Is that true?"

"In spades. Everyone knows that."

"Well, let's examine my definition more closely. If you think about it, the 'what' in what you deliver is about a total experience of your company. It's not confined to your products. It doesn't stop at performance under your warranties. It's every conceivable interaction that people have with every person or department in your company concerning every subject. They all comprise your Brand. Think holistically, Ben. Everything is connected to everything. It's all one Brand message."

Ben was beginning to see shades of gray in Brandon's comments. Brandon couldn't be right. Ben had spent too many hours developing and testing his theory. It worked. He owned it. Some outside consultant he never heard of wasn't going to waltz in here and undo his work, was he? The cloud of gray got bigger as Ben began to think holistically. *Wait a minute. Screw this holistic crap. Where is it written that a company is a holistic entity? Who says? Brandon Strong? Screw Brandon Strong. But Joe's a smart guy. He wouldn't have brought Brandon in unless Brandon knew what he was talking about. And, by the way, Joe is my boss. He deserves a little respect.*

Brandon went on. "Ben, in your definition, you talked about Brand depreciation occurring when you do things to tarnish your Brand and when you send messages that drive people away. What did you have in mind?"

Ben was ready. "I mean things like touting a particular feature in one of our blenders, and when people buy the product, the feature doesn't work properly. Or announcing a new, hot color for our toasters, but we can't ship it on time and the stores don't have the color in stock when people go to buy it. Those are examples of tarnishing our Brand. And as far as sending negative messages, I'm thinking about bad demographic research that results in touting a product feature in our ad campaign that our target customer doesn't want and won't pay for."

"Isn't something like that remote?" asked Brandon.

"It happened to us earlier this year with our new mid-price iron, just a couple of months after the acquisition. Remote or not, we did it. It was a nightmare."

"Good examples," said Brandon. "Let me give you another one. Suppose you have a customer, a retailer who has sold your products for some years. And this retailer falls behind on his account. They claim there are extenuating circumstances. They talk to your credit people to negotiate extended terms. Your credit people cite your credit policies and say no. Then they proceed with legal action against the retailer. You ultimately work out a payment program and avoid litigation. They act as if everything is OK, but they de-emphasize your line. You lose sales in that region. It doesn't end there. The still-disgruntled retailer tells other retailers about your lack of loyalty and your inflexibility. Some other dealers who used to carry your line exclusively start to carry other lines—just to hedge their bets. They explain to you that they love you and love your products. Everything's fine. They just need a more diversified offering to better serve their customers. Sales start to flatten."

Ben jumped in. "It's very funny that you cite that kind of example. A year ago we had almost that exact situation occur with a strong regional retail chain in the Northeast. Our credit manager, who reports to me, wanted to take the rigid position you cited. Our regional sales manager prevailed upon him to stretch our policies and work with the company. They had some one-time, extraordinary expenses that put them in a cash bind. They'd been a loyal customer and a strong voice for our products for years. I initially favored taking the hard line and demanding payment. But our credit manager and I allowed ourselves to be swayed by our sales manager. I lost sleep for a week agonizing and second-guessing myself. In the end, our salespeople were right. The company performed exactly as they promised. We saved a valuable customer who's even more loyal today because we helped them through a rough time."

Brandon spoke. "Don't you think that what you did was an integral part of your Brand?" he asked.

"No, I don't. It was a credit decision, pure and simple. It has nothing to do with our Brand."

"Remember, I asked you to think holistically. What if your marketing people put out an advertising campaign that conveyed the message, 'We're a great company. We'll work with you through good times and bad. You'll never have a better friend.' And then you took the hard line approach and demanded payment. Would that create a Brand issue?"

"Wait a minute," said Ben, between sips of coffee. "I think I see what you're driving at. It doesn't matter who it comes from. All of us send Brand messages, according to your definition of Brand."

"Is there anything that you find fault with in my definition?"

Ben took a three-sip pause before answering. "No, I really can't see anything wrong with it. But, if I use your definition in running my areas of responsibility, I can see where everyone has to be wearing two hats: their functional hats and their Brand hats."

"Is that a bad thing?" asked Brandon.

Ben thought again. "No, I can't see where it is. Bad, that is. But I'm having a little trouble getting my arms around this holistic concept of yours. I tend to see things more linearly, more separated, and more black-and-white. But when I think about it, you actually make sense. After all, our customers don't sit down and categorize their opinion of us based on where their experiences occur. They have a total experience, and they form a composite opinion, or as you say, a set of beliefs. And from those beliefs, they form expectations. In the final analysis, I guess that aligns with my definition of our Brand being about bringing in revenue. It doesn't matter if a customer does or doesn't do business with us because of our credit policies, or because of some product feature. You're calling our Brand that total experience. I can start to see that."

All of a sudden, Ben started laughing. "You know, Brandon," he said, "I've known you for all of twenty minutes. In that short time, I'm about to give up my definition of our Brand, one that I've spent years developing. I've never done that with anyone about anything, ever. But what you say makes sense. I don't know why we hadn't thought about it that way ourselves."

"Well," said Brandon, "I think there's a lot of tradition and common practice that gets in the way. Besides that, there's a body of knowledge built up in every functional area of business that mandates the need for everyone to specialize, to become narrower and deeper in their own field. Manufacturing people need to be better at manufacturing. Finance and accounting people need to be better at that. And so on. There's a proliferation of information in every field coming at us so fast that it's impossible to keep up. So we just never look up, never examine alternatives.

"Ben, I don't think you have to entirely discard your definition of your Brand. But it might shift—from a definition to a means of measuring Brand effectiveness."

Ben sipped, thought for a moment, and then spoke. "I'm not so concerned about that yet. I'm thinking back to your example of the credit situation with a customer. Are you suggesting that our people should roll over and make bad management decisions because they might seem justified in supporting our Brand? Do all our customers get a waiver on prompt payment of their account because they might bad-mouth us if we run a tight credit ship? I shudder to think about what that would do to our cash flow."

"Not at all," said Brandon. "Being sensitive to your Brand doesn't mean you forget the rules of business or allow yourself to be intimidated into making bad decisions. You can, however, make tough decisions with compassion. You can explain the reasons for your decisions with some empathy. You can help other people see things from your perspective, just as you attempt to see from theirs.

"Ben, tell me, doesn't at least one of your Core Values talk to your customers' success?"

"Absolutely."

"Well, doesn't living that Value relate to promoting the strength of your Brand? Seems to me that delivering a comprehensive experience of excellence enhances your Brand and also has you living your Core Values."

"Yes, of course it does," Ben said. "You know, Brandon, now that you bring up our Core Values, it seems like we have them, but they're tucked away in a desk drawer somewhere and only brought out for special occasions; like a crisis; or someone's annual performance review. You know what I mean, Joe?" he said, turning to his boss. "We don't focus on them every day for the small stuff."

"Well, perhaps we can focus on them as this project continues," Joe replied. "We'll see."

"In the meantime," said Ben, "I can see where my people are going to need some new skills and sensitivities if we're going to focus on performing according to your definition of our Brand. That's going to mean training. I don't know how we're set up for that, or if we can find the resources in this year's budget. Things are tight right now."

"Ben, you're getting ahead of the game. First of all, it may not require nearly as much training as you might think. And the training may not be as formal as you might imagine. Much of it has to do with raising awareness. So the cost will probably be lower than you think. But let's not even go there just yet. Let me tell you this, the entire management team is going to have on off-site retreat in about a week. I'd like you to think about a couple of things to prepare for it."

"What would you like from me?" asked Ben.

"I'd like you to think about all the times and in what contexts people in your area have any direct or indirect contact with your customers, end users, and vendors. Document those kinds of interactions. Then, think about and write down how you think those interactions can affect their total experience of dealing with your company."

"Yes, of course. You're looking for the impact on our Brand. Right?"

"Right," said Brandon.

"Is it OK if I include some of my people in this process? And do you want a written report of some kind before the retreat?"

"By all means bring your people in; it's a great idea. But no, you don't need to write a report. But definitely bring your notes to the retreat, with copies for everyone."

"You know, Brandon," Ben continued between coffee sips, "operating with this definition is going to take everyone in my area from 'scorekeepers' as you described before, to players. That's a big cultural shift."

"I know. But Ben, you like everything measured. And you love accountability. Here's a chance to practice what you preach."

Ben laughed. "Hey, Brandon. I'm a finance guy. I analyze and report. Accountability for operating results is for other people, not me. But, you know, there is a little adrenalin rush when you know you're playing and not just being a spectator or scorekeeper. It's a good thing, I think. I just have to get used to it. So will my people. And some of them are going to be scared shitless. Even though it seems like a small change."

"We'll cover that ground soon enough," said Brandon. "Are you OK with the assignment I gave you?"

"It's great. I'll get started as soon as we're finished here."

"Well, I believe we're finished. See you in about a week, Ben. Thanks for your time and your insights."

As Joe and Brandon left Ben's office and headed back for Joe's, Brandon spoke.

"Joe, thanks for just sitting there and mostly observing. I could sense several times that you wanted to jump in and didn't. Nice restraint."

"Several times, it took everything I had to keep my mouth shut. I'm actually quite proud of myself. But I learned some things. And I have lots of questions."

"Great. Why don't we have lunch brought in to your office and debrief while we eat? I think we're ready to have a progress discussion before we meet the others."

"Am I going to get indigestion or heartburn doing this over lunch?" Joe asked.

"I don't think so," Brandon laughed, "but let's go see. Oh, and don't order anything spicy."

Chapter 5

Lunching On Questions

As they entered Joe's office, Joe made a beeline for his Eames chair. He needed to reestablish some sense of command. The morning interviews had left him feeling like a stranger in his own home. In the blink of an eye, Brandon had been able to elicit some truths from three trusted members of Joe's team that had eluded Joe for months, if not years.

Brandon instantly sensed what Joe was feeling. He smiled.

"Don't worry, you're still the boss," he said as Joe plopped into his ceremonial seat of power.

"Am I that obvious?" asked Joe.

Joe had called Alice while they were walking back to his office to order lunch: a roast beef sandwich for Brandon and a tuna sandwich for himself. When lunch arrived they moved to the small conference table.

Joe sat, intensively staring at his sandwich as if he expected the tuna to speak. Brandon ate quietly, allowing Joe to have his contemplative moment. He knew that Joe had to be the one to break the silence. To Joe, the next five minutes seemed like an hour.

Finally, Joe spoke. "I don't know where to begin. How could I not see what's been happening right under my nose? The culture war going on with our new divisions, the breakdown in communication, the different ways our own leaders see our Brand. Where the hell have I been?"

"Don't be too hard on yourself," said Brandon. "Not yet, anyway. We're just getting started. There'll be plenty of time for analysis, introspection, and self-flagellation, if that's what you're into. Let me just say this for now. You are witnessing disparate parts operating within a framework, and the framework itself does not have a defined identity. It's as if you were conducting an orchestra of talented musicians, but each one is playing his or her individual melody and not harmonizing to create a great symphony."

"Great. Metaphorically you're telling me that I'm leading a bunch of talented people who are not working well together. I need real-life solutions, not metaphors. What the hell do you suggest I do about it?"

"Let's keep it simple for now," said Brandon. "We still need to talk to more of your people and digest what everyone has to say, so that we can form a more accurate picture of your culture, your collective behavior, and the results you're getting. But here's what we've heard so far. There's no universal agreement about the definition of your Brand. Everyone sees it somewhat differently. Mark, Manny, and Ben each see their roles, responsibilities, and connections to contributing to the quality and public perception of your Brand differently. I haven't heard much in the way of anyone connecting how they support your Brand to your Core Values. And no one has talked about coordinating their respective areas of control and responsibilities with one another to create a more unified Brand image among your customers. Silo mentalities around control are still the order of the day. Your people hoard information to preserve their personal power rather than sharing it for the common good. That's what I meant when I talked about disparate parts and an orchestra made up of soloists who don't create a unified body of work. And we haven't even touched on the cultural chemistry between your original, high-end line and your new mid-price product divisions. It seems to me that you have a very strong we-versus-they atmosphere in that area."

Joe heard the message clearly and silently accepted its intellectual sensibility. Yet he still had some reservations about Brandon's views as to the pervasiveness of everyone's direct connection to their Brand.

"Wait a minute," said Joe. "I hear what you're saying. And a lot of it makes sense to me. But as far as our Brand goes, I don't think we've reached crisis proportions here. Manny might not see his direct involvement in our Brand the same way that Mark does, but he does his part to build great products, minimize defects and returns, and deliver on time. He understands the importance of our reputation. And I thought Ben had a productive financial take on our Brand, even if he didn't get the full holistic perspective you described. And when you explained your definition, he came around pretty quickly. No resistance. And let's remember we're talking to people with specialized functional responsibilities. It almost sounds like you're trying to turn everyone into a marketing person."

"If you fully understand the implications of my definition of a Brand," Brandon responded, "you should see that supporting and strengthening your Brand involves so much more than marketing. But there is more going on here than a discussion of my definition of your Brand."

"Like what?"

"You've been in the business world for quite a while," said Brandon. "You've had experiences and built beliefs over many years. In the course of that time, you've come to regard certain kinds of dysfunctional behavior as normal. You just accept that it's the way things and people are. And you're OK with it."

"Again, like what?"

"Like the fact that because marketing and manufacturing and finance people are naturally going to see things differently, that being political and manipulative to have their point of view prevail is normal, and, more importantly, acceptable."

"Well, as long as it doesn't get out of control, what's wrong with that? It's just people being competitive."

"For starters, it's counterproductive and expensive," Brandon said. "And it becomes normal if you allow it to thrive. But, in truth, it's poisonous. Politics triumphs over creativity. Bringing divergent perspectives to bear on a given set of issues, however, isn't the same thing as sabotaging someone else's position. It's impossible to see the value of a different perspective if your only goal is personal victory."

"And you think that's what's happening here?"

"You betcha'," said Brandon. "It's mostly civilized, but it's still toxic. And it strengthens everyone's perceived need to maintain absolute control of his own silo of power and to keep transparency to a minimum. More significantly, it prevents people from embracing this holistic definition of your Brand. And that, my friend, could ultimately kill you in the marketplace."

"Don't you think you're being just a wee bit melodramatic for effect?" asked Joe.

"What I think is that this is a good stopping point in our discussion for now. I want you to keep what we've talked about in your consciousness as we finish the interviews and prepare for our retreat. It will give you another filter through which to hear whatever it is we're going to hear. You and I will have time later to dig deeper, learn more, and get a better handle on the issues and opportunities in front of you."

"Fair enough," said Joe, glancing at his watch as he spoke. "Besides, it's time for our next interview. I'm anxious to test my new listening filter," he said with a good-natured grin.

Chapter 6

New Product Development –
Passion Unleashed

The new product-development group had its own wing. The space they occupied was laid out like a wheel with a large hub, the nerve center of the division, and six spokes emanating from it, each spoke containing several small "brainstorming" rooms mixed within rows of cubicles housing the designers. Desi Concepcion, the Vice President of Product Development and the creative force behind Kitchen Sculpture, occupied the hub. Attached to his office were three "grOOp rooms," as Desi liked to spell them—one large and two smaller ones. Desi's office had giant whiteboards for walls, with a large smart board embedded in the center of one wall. Each wall was filled with rainbows of concept drawings, doodles of ideas scribbled randomly between the drawings and a collection of seemingly unconnected to-do lists with names attached to them, all scattered throughout the room. To the casual observer, it could easily have been seen as the inside of a mental institution housing incurable crazies. But design genius lived there.

Desi was immaculate and sleek, a human embodiment of his designs. He was in his early fifties, a slender six feet tall, clean-shaven, and black hair elegantly streaked with brushstrokes of gray. His face was angular, and his dark eyes housed a laser intensity. He eschewed the corporate look in favor of casual elegance. Today he wore slightly faded True Religion jeans; a crisp, white Armani shirt loosely draped his body, the rolled-up sleeves revealing a classic Movado black and rose gold watch. Charcoal Prada loafers with no socks completed the look.

"Desi," said Joe, "I'd like you to meet Brandon Strong. He's a highly recommended consultant working with us to better understand and strengthen our Brand."

"Great. Let me make it easy for you, Brandon," he said, smiling and dramatically extending his hand. "There's nothing wrong with our Brand that can't be fixed by giving me the resources I've been begging for to strengthen the designs in our mid-price lines."

As he spoke, Desi fixed his laser stare on Brandon, as if that alone could burn his request into reality. Brandon eyed Desi blankly and never flinched. Joe turned his head away from both men, smiled, and said nothing. He would let Desi have his moment.

Desi was born to design. He saw everything through the eyes of an anthropomorphic sculptor. He loved to turn his objects into living, working "beings" with feelings and personalities. He struggled with accepting the financial constraints imposed on him by the practical needs of a business. He recognized requirements like profit and return on investment, but they were far down on his list of what mattered in life.

Desi's ego was beyond big and interestingly complex. He would demonstrate inspiring compassion and sensitivity to designers struggling to find their own creative fires. He never talked down to them, never lost patience, and always gave them credit for their ideas, even when those ideas ended up in the scrap heap. It was a vital part of the creative process, he would say. There was no such thing as failure, only learning. His people revered him. He was their Dalai Lama and Bruce Lee with a side order of Picasso thrown in.

But Desi had another persona, unleashed on those outside his creative sphere. His demeanor with people he deemed unappreciative of creativity showed as much tolerance as the citizens of Salem displayed toward suspected witches. His verbal attacks, swift and venomous, earned him the nickname Cobra. It was not a badge of honor, but Desi wore it as if it were.

The conflicts between Desi and almost every other executive were predictable, and came to be accepted as one of the cultural norms at Kitchen Sculpture. That was because Joe allowed the conflicts and, over time, had become an effective negotiator and mediator. He was adept at balancing the organization's creative needs with its fluctuating physical and financial resources and, in the process, optimizing results. In the course of hammering out direction and strategies, there were many bloody noses but no serious injuries. Joe's leadership skills had always delivered great results. Only recently had the winds of change shifted and blown little gusts of doubt into some people's minds. Desi was one of those people.

"Tell me more," said Brandon.

"You really want to hear me out, or are you just patronizing me, like the rest of the Neanderthals around here?"

"Whoa," said Brandon. "Is that what you really think of everyone else around here?"

"At times, yes. And some times more than others. Like now, for instance."

"I want to hear more. But I'd like to frame your comments in a somewhat different context. Let's talk about your issues and observations as a part of what is the reality of your Brand."

"I'm not sure I understand."

"OK. I'm going to give you my definition of your Brand. And I'd like your response, taking into account your feelings about how you interact with your Brand and what others are doing to prevent you from fully contributing to its strength."

"Go for it," said Desi. "This should be interesting, but I don't think it's going to change my beliefs about our Brand."

"Well, then, please tell me your beliefs about your Brand. How would you define your Brand?"

"Our Brand is the total feeling that people get when they see our products, use our products, and react to their experience of our products. It's a visceral thing, not an advertising message. Our sales and marketing people—the pimps of promise—are always crowing about their 'Branding programs,' and building Brand awareness. That's just the wrapping. The real deal is inside the box—our products and what they deliver. Different emotions come into play when people experience our products. They get a sensual pleasure from using them because our products don't just perform, they interact with their owners; people get a tactile pleasure from simply touching and feeling the sculptural artistry in our products; and they get a sense of pride when they show off our products to their friends. Our products are seen as status symbols. That, my friend, is our Brand. When we deliver the experience I just described, our Brand is strong. When we don't, our Brand weakens. That is the message I drive home to our designers and our technologists every day."

As his words poured out, Desi became more passionate with each phrase. His final words hit Brandon's ears with the force of a Billy Graham sermon. Desi believed. Desi would not be swayed—at least not easily.

Joe could no longer remain silent. "Desi, the pimps of promise? What's up with your attitude about our sales and marketing people?"

"I know they play a role," Desi answered. "I just think those guys believe the sun rises and sets on them. Their skills are about making promises and creating expectations. There's no real substance in that. Our best Brand ambassadors are our products themselves, not the hype that goes into them. We spend enough money on hot air to put the Goodyear Blimp into permanent orbit."

"But Desi," said Brandon, "isn't having a widely known name an integral part of your Brand? And doesn't the name recognition a Branding campaign creates help drive your sales?"

"Maybe initially, but we can only sustain our name and our sales if we deliver the experience people want and expect," said Desi. "And we do that with our products, not with words."

Brandon stood silently for a long moment, partly to show Desi the respect that his passion warranted, and partly to let Desi calm down enough to hear another's words.

"A thoughtful and heartfelt definition," said Brandon. "I think it defines you and your passion for your products. Let me give you a slightly different definition, one that I'd like you to think about before you respond. Here it is. *'Your Brand is a widely held set of beliefs and expectations about what you deliver and how you deliver it, validated by customers' experiences.'*"

Desi turned away from Brandon and began to pace slowly back and forth across the length of the room, his head down and his hands shoved into his pockets. Brandon and Joe silently watched. After five full minutes he just stopped, turned, and walked back toward Brandon.

"OK, I've thought about it," said Desi. "Brandon, I think your definition implies the inclusion of a bunch of people and activities into the mix that don't have anything to do with our Brand. They're just peripheral activities that go on in any business but don't have a damn thing to do with a Brand."

"Give me an example."

Desi was heating up as he spoke. "Like, what the hell does anyone or anything in our accounting department have to do with our Brand? What does our shipping department do that defines our Brand? Please. Let's get real here. Do you actually believe for one nanosecond that a shipping clerk can affect our Brand in the same way as a great product design can?"

"Great question. Let's explore it. Suppose that every person in every area of the company except yours did exceptional work. Your product designs sucked and nothing performed as advertised. What happens to your Brand? What happens to sales and profits?"

"Brandon, no disrespect intended, but this is infantile, and you're boring me. You know damn well what would happen."

"Humor me," said Brandon. "Now suppose you put out great product designs with highly advanced functionality. But shipments were consistently late, orders were frequently wrong, and inventories were not properly balanced, so back orders were necessary most of the time. In addition, manufacturing was sloppy, and product malfunctions occurred regularly. Dealers were unhappy, and too many customers were furious and demanded refunds. Desi, whaddya think, do we have a Brand problem here?"

"No, we don't. I see where you're going, but no, we don't have a Brand problem. We have other operational issues, like manufacturing process problems, training, shipping department breakdowns to address, et cetera, et cetera. Those can be big problems, but they're not Brand problems."

"Let's go back to my definition," said Brandon. "Think about the concept of 'what you deliver and how you deliver it.' And let's think in terms of your customers' total experience as seen through their eyes. You were passionate when you described the feelings that your customers have when they used your products. Isn't it true that your customers would have strong feelings about every other aspect of their experience with your company? In my scenario you'd be delivering great-looking products that didn't perform and arrived late. Too often, they didn't work properly and it took too long to correct the mistakes. And when your customers' friends ask them about your products, your customers will tell them that they look good but don't work, and that they didn't get what they ordered. Do you believe that your customers are going to parse the situation the way we just did to isolate where the problems occurred? I think they're just going to say that your Brand stinks. What do you think?"

For the first time since the meeting began, a hint of uncertainty clouded Desi's eyes. His laser-glare softened. He first looked at Brandon, and then turned toward Joe. Before speaking, he turned back to Brandon.

"This might sound incredibly stupid, but I never really looked at our Brand through our customers' eyes the way you just did, Brandon. I think I always saw the myriad of potential problems we could encounter. I just saw them as disconnected from our Brand. But I can see how a customer would not make that distinction. Wow. Something so basic and I just flat-out missed it. Shit. Joe, I feel like taking a break to go down the hall and slit my wrists."

Joe broke in before Brandon could respond. "Desi, don't think for a minute that you're alone with that feeling. Notice that I haven't said much this whole time. I wanted you and Brandon to explore this area without my opinions or biases intruding. But just for the record, I started this process in pretty much the same place as you. Have you really changed your opinion so quickly?"

"Joe, you know me as well as I know myself. So you know I have strong views about everything. And I usually don't let anything—especially the facts—get in my way. I'm used to telling people what they should and should not like. But there's something about the way Brandon presented this perspective—looking through the eyes of the end user—that just hit me differently. I know he's not the first to bring up some of the stuff he talked about. I just felt it in a new way. Who knows? I might go back to my original position after I sleep on it. But right now, it all makes sense, and I'm willing to look at things in a new way. So you guys better take it while it's here."

"We'll take it," said Joe.

"So where are we going with this?" said Desi. "What else do you need from me?"

"Here's what I'd like you to do," said Brandon. "Think about the situations you've encountered recently that have made it difficult for you to strengthen your Brand in the way you thought you could. And I don't mean you personally, but rather your entire team. Chronicle the situations in writing with as much detail as you can recall."

"That'll be easy. There is one major area that has been bugging me ever since we made the acquisitions of the mid-price product line companies."

"Oh no, let's not go down that path right now," said Joe. "We'll be here all night."

"Well, you guys opened the door. But I'll wait until the right time to explode through it. And Brandon, thanks for the opportunity."

"Good," said Brandon. "I'm anxious to hear—at the right time."

"And when will that be?"

"We're going to have an executive retreat in about a week. Everyone will have a lot to weigh in on. Could be fun, in a serious kind of way. Will you be ready?"

"Count on it," said Desi. "Count on it."

Chapter 7

Awakenings

Brandon and Joe walked pensively down the hall toward their next meeting, heads down and brows furrowed, each processing what they had just heard and felt.

After several moments, Brandon said softly, "Wow. Seems like something is really bothering Desi, and I think it goes beyond what he revealed during our little discussion. What's bugging him?"

"I think I know. Actually, I'm pretty sure I know. And you're right; it goes beyond what came out in our meeting. I thought I had a better handle on the situation involving Desi and some of the other execs as well, but I guess I don't. Now, I'm concerned. You can see that Desi is just as emotional as he is creative. I don't mind that he gets a little melodramatic about things; that's just Desi. I think everyone else is OK with it, too. But he usually gets whatever he feels off his chest and he's done with it—whatever the 'it' seems to be. But when he stays in his funk mood, his creativity suffers. It's contagious, and his people pick up on it. Then their creativity goes south."

"So what is it? What's bugging Desi?"

"I'm surprised that you don't just automatically know, you being so 'highly' recommended and all," Joe said, with an eyebrow raised and a sly smile.

Brandon laughed. "I'm not a mind reader, Joe—just perceptive. If I could read minds, we wouldn't need these meetings, would we?"

"Yeah, I know. I just had to jab you a little. I could tell you what I think is going on with Desi, but since we're having our retreat in a week, I want it to come out there, with everyone else in the room, because it involves more than Desi. And I don't want to influence your thinking before you experience the entire group dynamic in action. I'm definitely concerned about Desi, but it'll keep for a week."

"But Joe, you just said you thought you had a handle on a situation, and it turns out you don't. Don't you think it would help to let me in on it now?"

"Let me just say that we're all still in the middle of big cultural changes as a result of our three acquisitions. Right this minute, I'm OK with letting it come out next week."

"OK," said Brandon. "You're the boss. Let's go see Erika."

Chapter 8

Information Technology – A Break From Tradition

Erika Opensource, Vice President and Chief Technology Officer, was the youngest and least "corporate" executive at Kitchen Sculpture. She was twenty-eight years old, but her perpetual semi-frown made her look ten years older. She was quantitatively brilliant, quick, humorless in the presence of non-techies, showed little interest in developing her interpersonal skills, and maddeningly multi-tasked except when explicitly ordered to stop. She was trim, with short, straight, dark brown hair, eyes to match, and wore no makeup. She could have looked attractive if she cared, but she didn't. When it came to technology, she was all business all the time. Small talk, for her, was out of the question. Yet, with all the behavioral "Do Not Enter" signs she posted, most people liked and respected her. She was authentic, honest, and ethical. With Erika, candor mattered. She gave it and took it with equal comfort.

"Hello, Erika," said Joe. "I want to introduce you to Brandon Strong. Brandon is a highly recommended consultant that I've brought in to help us better understand and strengthen our Brand."

"OK," said Erika. She looked at Joe as she spoke, and if she acknowledged Brandon at all, it was only out of the corner of her eye.

"Hi Erika," said Brandon, extending his hand. "It's nice to meet you."

"Right." Erika stood erect, firm as a statue. She looked Brandon in the eye but made no move to shake his hand. She was being typical Erika. "What does this Brand stuff have to do with me?"

"More than you might think, Erika. Let's start with this. What's your definition of your Brand?"

"Who cares? I have nothing to do with our Brand. Is that it? Because I have some projects to get back to."

Joe sat back, silently laughing through his disappointment. He expected more professionalism from Erika. But he couldn't stifle his amusement at how Brandon, for the first time since they met, was thrown completely off guard by her unwillingness to engage.

The moment didn't last long. Brandon knew he needed to gain control—and quickly. "Erika, for starters, I care. Joe cares. And every other executive cares, or soon will. That's the whole purpose of why we're looking to strengthen your Brand. So cut me some slack. I would never try to tell you how to do your job. So please, let's not start our discussion with you telling me how to do mine. Fair enough?" Brandon's sudden testiness registered with Erika. Joe's antenna went up as well.

Now it was Erika's turn to retreat. She liked Brandon's candor. He said what she would have said if the situation were reversed. "Fair enough." She sounded sincere yet not engaged. It was Erika being Erika. If it wasn't about technology, she was civil but indifferent.

"OK," she conceded, "you want to hear my definition of our Brand. Right?"

"Right."

"Our Brand is about connection." Silence followed.

"That's it?" said Brandon.

"Pretty much."

"I need more. What do mean by connection?"

"I'm talking about how people become loyal to us, to our products, how they want to engage with us and tell us what they like and don't like, how they come to trust us, how they want to be able to tell us what new features they want, what new products they want, how they like or don't like how it is to do business with us, how they want to have a dialogue with us and not just have advertising messages shoved down their throats. Connection, dude."

"Wow. You seem angry. Are you angry?"

"I used to be. Now I just don't care."

Joe listened intently. He knew Erika had become more withdrawn of late. He had just assumed it was her nature. But she'd never displayed this level of anger, at least not in front of him. What the hell was going on here? Another surprise he didn't need.

Brandon let the moment percolate. When he sensed that Erika's blood pressure had sufficiently receded, he spoke. "Erika, what do you do when you're not working?"

"What? What kind of question is that?"

"A personal one. I'm curious."

"I ride my bike."

"Ten speed, beach bike, mountain bike?"

"A Harley," said Erika.

Joe had a sudden attack of stereotype conflict. He felt as if he'd just learned that his favorite nun secretly drove the getaway car for a gang of bank robbers.

Brandon took it all in stride. "Interesting," he said. "What do you get out of it?"

"A sense of freedom. And peace. And solitude. When I'm riding either alone or with my club friends, I'm in a different world. We can relate and interact without saying a word to each other. It's like we know what everyone's thinking without talking. I love that feeling. We're all on one level. There's no hierarchy. Everybody's opinion matters equally. Sometimes I imagine that if there is a heaven, that's how it would feel."

Joe had not yet recovered from his Harley shock. "Erika, you're riding with a gang?" he asked.

"It's a club, Joe, not a gang. I'm not a member of the Hell's Angels. Relax. We ride together, we eat together, and we participate in some charity events together. I'm not a threat to society," she said with an amused smile. *How could Joe be so innocent?*

"Interesting hobby," said Brandon. "Anything else you do in your spare time?"

"Yes."

"What?"

"I spend as much time as I can online, looking for and reading about new technologies related to social media."

"You spend all your working hours immersed in technology, and yet you spend some portion of your free time diving into more technology. Why?"

"Because I like the human interactions and the virtual relationships that are possible through social media. I can feel connected and, at the same time, be alone. That's a kind of intimacy that is comfortable for me. And from a technical standpoint, I love learning about the open-source technologies driving that world of virtual intimacy and connection. I'm a closet 'mashable' junkie."

"Wow. Mashable and motorcycles. You're an eclectic mix, all right." Brandon grinned.

For the first time since the meeting began, Erika smiled. "I never thought about it that way. You might have a point."

Joe was finally coming out of his shock-induced stupor. "Erika," he said, "you and I never discussed your personal interests. I just thought it was none of my business. I'm sorry if I seemed so shocked."

"Joe, it's not exactly like no one in the world knows. I've put up lots of photos on my Facebook page and on Flickr. I write posts about the stuff I do. But I do that for my friends, and I don't share any of that information with anyone who isn't a friend—online or off. I like you, but we're not real friends. So I'd like this conversation kept between us."

"You have my word," said Joe. Brandon nodded in agreement.

"OK," said Brandon. "Let's get back to discussing your Brand. Erika, you gave me your definition of your Brand. Now let me give you mine. *Your Brand is a widely held set of beliefs and expectations about what you deliver and how you deliver it, validated by customers' experiences.* Think about it for a few minutes, and tell me your reaction to it."

Erika needed only a minute. "Your definition is much broader than mine. It brings into play a lot of people and functions that I don't interact with. I relate to the aspects of what you call our Brand where I feel I can make a contribution. Other than that, I really don't think about our Brand in the course of my work. I guess you have a point. But I don't see how it involves me or my team and the work we do. So I'm back to my original question. Why are we talking? What's the purpose?"

"Erika, a few minutes ago, you gave me a passionate description of what you think is your Brand. When I asked you if you were angry, you said that you used to be but you no longer care. Why don't you care? What made you stop?"

"I stopped caring because after knocking my head against a wall trying to present new ideas to Mark, and to some extent to you, Joe, I realized that my opinion about anything other than handling data has no value in this place. So I figure that since you guys are going to do what you want to do, and you're not willing to look at new ways of connecting to customers, then why should I give a shit? So I stopped. I do my job, collect my paycheck, and I look for real fulfillment outside of this place. Kitchen Sculpture gets my brain but not my heart. Sorry Joe, but that's the way it is."

Suddenly Erika sat rigidly upright and shifted her gaze from Joe to Brandon and back to Joe. "Whoa," she said. "I can't believe I just said what I just said. I'm not sorry; I'm, like, blown away. Brandon, there's something going on with you that makes me willing to be honest and out there. What is it?"

"How do you feel, now that you've said all that?" asked Brandon.

"Relieved. Like a weight just came off my back. And maybe a little scared, as in I'm suddenly about to lose my job."

"What about you, Joe? How do you feel?" asked Brandon.

Joe sat silently, looking mostly at Erika, with a few sideways glances at Brandon. "Well," he began slowly, still looking intently at Erika, "I appreciate hearing the truth. Although I have to tell you I'm not too crazy about the content of that truth. Erika, I knew you had become more withdrawn over the last several months, but I had no idea it was because you felt the way you just described."

"Joe, you never asked me. How come?"

"Look, we all have our personal lives and our personal problems. I don't like to get into people's private situations. And while I expect everyone to cope with their own ups and downs and not let things interfere with their performance, sometimes they do. So that's what I thought was happening with you. Whatever it was, I figured it was personal."

"Joe, you know I've never let anything personal get in my way at work. I'm totally blown away at how you didn't see the possibility that something here had freaked me out. You were in on some of the arguments that Mark and I had over his unwillingness to develop a serious social media presence and to revamp our website design. You watched my frustration grow to the breaking point. Or at least I thought you did. I guess I was wrong."

"I watched without seeing and listened without hearing," Joe said, shaking his head in amazement. "I apologize. I guess I was so focused on the content of what you, Mark, and everyone else had to say that I didn't pay attention to the energy and the emotions you guys were expressing. Hell, in retrospect, we could have had those meetings by text message. That's no excuse; just an explanation."

"I accept your apology, as long as I still have my job." She smiled sheepishly.

"Of course you still have your job. It's my conduct that I'm worried about. I should be able to read you—and everyone else. It seems I haven't been doing it very well for the last several months." He paused to think before continuing. "You know, I think the pressure that we've all been under since we completed the acquisitions is getting to us, and we're not aware of how it's creeping into our conduct with each other. It's like gaining five pounds a year for ten years. You wake up one morning and you see for the first time that you're fifty pounds overweight and you don't have a clue how you got there. But wait a minute," he stopped himself. "I'm getting us way off track. We're here to discuss our Brand."

"You're not as far off as you might think," said Brandon. "Let's go back to my definition—*what* you deliver and *how* you deliver it. Erika, you said that my definition was broader than yours and it involved other people and functions. Yet there are parts of your Brand that you can impact. They're not being addressed because your ideas have been rejected—tossed aside, perhaps because your executive team is under so much pressure they're not open to new ideas.

"But Erika, if your ideas about social media and website redesign were implemented, would they affect what you deliver and how you deliver it?"

"Of course they would," said Erika.

"How?"

"You're kidding, right?"

"No, I'm not."

"Having conversations *with* people rather than preaching *to* people can dramatically strengthen our relationships with end users and dealers who want to engage in that kind of dialogue. It can add a dimension to customer loyalty that goes way beyond our product designs and functionality. Right now, our customers' loyalty is based solely on our ability to stay at the cutting edge of artistic design and performance. That's good. But if we had that and in addition we had a twenty-first-century approach to building two-way relationships, we would be untouchable. Just my opinion. But what do I know? I'm just that nerdy chick who manages data and runs reports that our marketing geniuses request."

Joe started to respond, but Brandon jumped in first. "Erika, here's what I'd like you to do. Please put in writing your ideas as to how you think the things you've described can be developed and implemented to improve your Brand within the context of my definition. We're going to have a retreat in about a week for the sole purpose of better understanding and strengthening your Brand. I promise you a fair hearing regarding everything that you have to say about your Brand. You will be treated as a full-fledged member of the executive team—not as the nerdy chick who manages data."

"Amen," said Joe. "Erika, it's difficult for me to sit here and listen to your ideas and try to comprehend how and why you were shot down. I know that there are other financial and skills factors to consider in developing and executing the things you are recommending. But that doesn't excuse the way your ideas were dismissed. We, as a team, can and must do better. And we will."

"I'm good with all of this," said Erika. "I feel good about being heard. Brandon, Joe, do you want my ideas in the form of a report before this retreat you mentioned? Or should I just make copies and bring them to the retreat?"

"Just bring them to the retreat, with copies for everyone," said Brandon. "I'll give everyone a heads-up on the time and place. See you in about a week."

As Brandon and Joe left her office, Erika took her first relaxed breath in weeks. *I wonder,* she thought, *if those guys have a clue about what they're going to get from me in the way of suggestions. One thing was certain. Smug, self-confident Mr. Mark Selisman was going to have a shit fit.* She laughed out loud. It was not a happy laugh.

Chapter 9

Reflections And Assessments

"My capacity for the number of surprises I can handle in a single day is being tested," said Joe as he and Brandon headed over to Samantha Person's office for their final interview. "I have some angry people on my hands, and I didn't know it. Manny, Desi, and now Erika. Now I'm angry with myself for not knowing. You got right to the heart of things in a matter of minutes. I've been immersed in these issues for months and didn't see it. Brandon, have I lost it?"

"Don't be too hard on yourself," Brandon said, a touch of empathy in his voice. "For starters, you're as tangled in the trees as much as the people on your team. Your vantage point isn't any better than theirs. Secondly, you have no one but the guy in the mirror to talk to, so you're stuck with your own perspective, and you don't have a source for a second opinion. And third, you're operating in unknown waters as far as your personal experience goes. Take all that together, and you have the makings of a potpourri of puzzlement."

Joe stopped in his tracks and stared at Brandon. "A what did you say? A potpourri of puzzlement? So now I've gone from being just a little ol' CEO to becoming the maestro of mayhem, the titan of turmoil, the doyen of disorder?" Joe snorted a laugh. "Pardon me, but I need to find some feeble humor to help me get through this."

"*Feeble* is the operative word," said Brandon.

"Where are we going with all this?" asked Joe. "Everything we're doing is supposed to be focused on understanding and strengthening our Brand. Some of these anger issues seem far removed from our purpose. Desi, for example, is pissed off at the moment. But Desi is highly volatile all the time. He can hemorrhage if his morning latte is ten minutes late. He can also do his ode to joy dance if he sees a rosebud begin to open when he's conceiving a new design idea. That's Desi.

"Erika, on the other hand, troubles me more. Normally, her behavior is monochromatic all the time. She even speaks like a voice synthesizer. Yet, she had some interesting perspectives on, of all things, social media marketing. Who knew? And she felt shot down. She flat-out told me that her heart is not in her job. That is so at odds with our Core Values around ideas and creativity."

"What's your point?" asked Brandon.

"It feels like things are spinning out of control. We started our last two meetings talking about our Brand and we uncovered some issues that I'm not sure are relevant to what we're here to do. I'm not saying that those issues should be ignored. But shouldn't we focus on our Brand? I mean, where do these other elements take us? Disagreements about priorities and resource allocations and strategies are a normal part of life in any organization. What we just heard is, in my view, normal stuff. When you're working in an organization, things don't always go the way you want them to. When that happens, you suck it up and support the decisions that are made. You work as a team player."

"Is that what you really think?" Brandon asked skeptically. "That you have a couple of people who are just bent out of shape because a few things didn't go their way? And they're just throwing tantrums? Really?"

"Maybe. I'm not sure. I thought I knew them well. Especially Desi and Manny. Now I don't know. The bigger issue for me, right this minute, is how all this relates to strengthening our Brand."

"Joe, remember it's about *what* you deliver and *how* you deliver it. When what appears to be personal issues impact those elements, in addition to whatever else you've identified, your Brand is being weakened.

"Let's just look at Erika for a moment. You have, in her, a highly intelligent, capable person who thinks beyond the ones and zeroes, beyond the requests made of her by people whose creativity is imprisoned by the fear of stepping outside of their own experience. Those people can't see the possibilities that Erika sees. She's operating with a strong work ethic and an equally strong sense of futility. Imagine how much more she could contribute if your team welcomed her creative input? I'm not saying she necessarily has all the answers; some of her ideas may not be practical. But you guys aren't even conversationally exploring creative possibilities. How do you think that diminishes what you're delivering? Joe, your Brand is suffering from creative constipation."

"Uh-huh. First it's a potpourri of puzzlement, now it's creative constipation. Great. So what do we do? What do I do?"

"For right now, just keep an open mind. Take everything in and let it percolate. More of all these things will surface at our retreat. Creative tensions will erupt. Let them; it's part of the process. We're almost finished with the first part of our process. Let's go hear what Samantha has to say."

Chapter 10

Human Resources – Poise, Professionalism And Politics

Samantha Persons, Vice President of Human Resources, was the newest member of the senior management team. She came to Kitchen Sculpture from a Fortune 500 company a year ago. Samantha was in her mid forties. She exuded the stereotypically structured, formal polish associated with large organizations. Her posture was erect; her straight, dark blonde hair was tied in a ponytail with not a strand out of place. She wore black, straight-legged pants and a matching waist-length jacket over a short-sleeve, cream-colored, silk V-neck blouse, all balanced on black, two-inch heels. Her only jewelry was a pair of small, round, diamond-stud earrings (a gift from her parents), and a gold Cartier watch. Everything about her was medium: height, weight, complexion— everything but her ambition. That was extra-large. Her manner was friendly, and her smile seemed genuine, albeit a bit stiff. She had the air of an appealing sculpture perched in a gallery with a Look But Don't Touch sign on it.

Samantha left her large organization world because she felt unfulfilled, confined to manage the "traditional" functions of her role. She understood the importance of administering employee benefit programs, union contract negotiations, hiring, disciplining, and complying with a growing myriad of mind-numbing government regulations. Those things, however, prevented her from focusing on her real passion: training and career development. She loved teaching people the subtleties of interpersonal skills. She believed that mastery in those areas usually meant the difference between modest success and greatness. When she joined her previous company, she was given strong verbal assurances that the company's senior management shared her beliefs, and that she would be given the resources and the responsibility to build the programs needed to make those skills a mainstream element of their culture. It never came to pass. For five years she endured one excuse after another: budget cuts here, urgent priorities there, personnel changes somewhere else. It finally became too much. Samantha concluded that all the promises were lip service. Had she hit the glass ceiling or was she up against a culture that simply refused to embrace change? Either way, she would never be able to make a real difference; she was a corporate automaton, a well-paid cog in a wheel that turned at a glacial pace. Why, she wondered, did so many otherwise intelligent people believe that effective communication skills could just be assumed into existence? How did having a title and knowing how to assign tasks magically translate into real leadership?

She began to network under the radar, and found Kitchen Sculpture through an old colleague who knew Joe. For Samantha, this high-end, well-respected, growing entity represented an opportunity to spread her wings, dive into her passion, and make a real difference in the growth and stature of the organization. By doing so, she could build her own professional reputation and her importance to the organization, not to mention her bank account. Once she and Joe agreed on her new role at Kitchen Sculpture, she found a politically correct reason to resign from the Fortune 500 company. She left on good terms. No need to burn bridges.

Joe believed that Samantha represented the perfect opportunity to further differentiate Kitchen Sculpture by strengthening their interpersonal skills through training initiatives that few competitors could, or even wanted to, match.

Kitchen Sculpture's acquisitions of the mid-price products presented a short-term speed bump to that opportunity. Program integration was needed before cultural reform could proceed. That meant that Samantha was immersed in getting various benefit programs aligned, standardizing operating and administrative rules, and administering the layoffs needed to eliminate redundant positions. Long-term, Samantha would have a larger employee audience to coach and train. She knew that, and was willing to put her passion on hold and concentrate on immediate needs. Still, there were days when she had second thoughts about Kitchen Sculpture's commitment to skills training and questioned her decision to leave the relative stability of the Fortune 500 world she'd left behind.

As Joe and Brandon entered her office, Samantha got up from her desk and came around to greet them. Her handshake was firm and warm; her smile sent her usual friendly but not too personal message. Her office had "Neat Freak" written all over it.

"Samantha, I'd like you to meet Brandon Strong," said Joe. "He's a highly recommended consultant, and he's here to help us strengthen our Brand."

"It's nice to meet you. May I call you Brandon, or would you prefer Mr. Strong?"

"Brandon is just fine."

"How might I help you?" said Samantha with a smile. Polite, corporate-speak flowed as naturally from her as street jargon did from Manny Factura. *Two ends of the spectrum*, Brandon thought. *It'll be interesting to see how they interact in the cauldron of the retreat.*

"Samantha, I have a question for you. What is your definition of your Brand?"

Samantha's forehead wrinkled as she silently pondered the question for a few moments. "I know you have your reasons for asking me, but I'm not sure my answer will be particularly useful. Well, here goes. I think our Brand is all the things that the marketing and advertising world say about what a Brand is. A whole lot of awareness attributes that talk to name recognition and reputation. I strongly believe, however, that our Brand is also enhanced by our people's interpersonal skills, their abilities to listen productively to our customers, to communicate effectively, to exhibit empathetic understanding. All of these qualities directly affect peoples' attitudes about our company. They comprise the human component of our Brand. And of course, if we don't do those things well, our Brand can be damaged."

Brandon nodded. "Interesting. Now let me give you my definition of your Brand. *Your Brand is a widely held set of beliefs and expectations about what you deliver and how you deliver it, validated by customers' experiences.* Think about that for a moment and give me your reaction."

Samantha took only a few seconds. "I think our definitions are close, although I'm not entirely clear on what you mean by 'what we deliver.' We deliver products and customer service. And, of course how we interact with everyone in the course of delivering those things is the human side I referred to in my definition. So what else is there?"

"Samantha, do you see yourself and what you do as being a part of your Brand?"

"In an indirect sense, yes."

"What do mean by indirect?"

"My department and I don't directly interact with our customers or our suppliers or the public at large," she said. "We're invisible to those groups. Yet we play a role by giving people who do connect certain skills to help them excel at what they do. And in that process, we contribute to the strength of our Brand."

"What about other departments and people in the organization, like finance and manufacturing? Are they indirect as well?"

"I believe so," said Samantha, with just a hint of hesitation in her tone. Her political instincts sensed she might be headed down the wrong path. "I'm not suggesting that indirect contributions are not important, if that's what you're getting at. There's just a difference between being a coach and being a player."

"Do you see yourself as a coach?" asked Brandon.

"I do. And I think that's perfectly proper." There was a little defensiveness in her tone.

"Proper, perhaps," said Brandon. "But in this game, maybe a bit too safe and far too distant. In a business environment such as this one, there's a clear line between being a player and being a coach—someone who advises but who has no skin in the game. More importantly, being a 'coach' is more a style of leadership than a defined role. Samantha, you in particular, as a master of the subtleties of language, should understand that implicit in my definition of your Brand is that everyone in your organization is a player. There are no coaches and above all, no spectators.

"Let me give you a goofy illustration. Suppose you went to a retail store that carried Kitchen Sculpture products to buy an anniversary gift for a couple who was important in your life. The store was well designed, the displays were attractive, all the merchandise was high quality, the sales staff was attentive and knowledgeable, and they had just what you were looking for—the KS Blender. And of course they offered free gift-wrapping. It all seemed perfect. You purchased the blender. You were in a hurry and had more errands to run, so you left the item to be wrapped and planned to return in an hour to pick it up. You got delayed on your errands and now you were in a serious time bind. When you returned to the store, your gift was ready and waiting. You looked at it and cringed. It looked as if a three-year old child had wrapped it while immersed in a temper tantrum. You were infuriated. There was no time to fix it. The sales person apologized. The floor manager explained that the gift wrapper was new and hadn't been properly trained yet. The store was busy, and no one looked at your package before you returned. None of these excuses solved the problem or made you any happier. You stomped out of the store, utterly disgusted and embarrassed at the thought of presenting your gift in that state.

"How do you feel about the store? Will you go back? What will you tell people when they ask you if you know of a great gift store? What will you proactively tell people about your experience, especially while it's fresh in your mind?

"Meanwhile, back at the store, they are reviewing your unfortunate situation to determine how to correct it and prevent similar occurrences in the future. The gift wrapper throws up his hands in frustration. He explains that he told his supervisor that he had not been trained and that he had never before been a gift wrapper. He had begged for someone to train him before he went on the floor to work. His supervisor told him that their trainer was overloaded with other training priorities and would get to him as soon as possible. The trainer said that she did, in fact, give him some basic instruction and that she felt that gift-wrapping was not a big deal and that anyone with an IQ greater than his age should be able to figure it out. The trainer went on to say that she was not responsible for the quality of everyone's work; she was there to provide information, and that actual performance was each employee's personal responsibility.

"Who's right? Who's wrong? Do we fire someone? Do we allow the trainer's belief that she is just responsible for providing information to become the cultural norm? How might the trainer have approached this situation if she saw herself as a true 'player' and not as a coach or adviser? What kind of damage was done to the store's Brand as a result of this incident?

"And when it comes to Kitchen Sculpture, Samantha, do you see how its sales could suffer at that store? Not because of anything having to do with your products or service, but because someone didn't think it was important to train a gift wrapper. And because a trainer didn't see herself as an integral part of her store's Brand."

Samantha sat down for the first time since their meeting began. She stared into space as minutes that felt like hours ticked by. Finally, she looked first at Joe, then at Brandon.

"What are you thinking?" asked Brandon.

Samantha spoke slowly, measuring every word. "I think I am staring into a deep, churning pool of enormous opportunity. I have spent the last five years of my career being forced to sit on the sidelines and watch others play the real game. Joe, you and I discussed this at length before I joined the company. I now have the opportunity to become a real player, and I am unconsciously balking, retreating from the reality of actually making a difference. My God what a wake-up call. I am so embarrassed. Joe, I am truly sorry for my unconscious attitude."

"Samantha, you haven't done anything wrong, and you have nothing to apologize for," said Joe.

"Oh, yes I have and yes I do. I have been sitting back and blaming others—you in particular, Joe—for not giving me enough resources to begin our training initiatives. The whole time I've been behaving like a spectator, wanting things handed to me, not taking the initiative, not being creative in finding ways to help our people improve their interpersonal skills. I know I can do more if I just put my mind to it. Nobody ever told me not to be creative. That's on me.

"Brandon, thank you for smacking me between the eyes with your two-by-four and waking me up. I've been sleepwalking through this part of my job since I got here. I've used all the excuses that worked at my prior company to keep me from being resourceful and making things happen. I've become so unconsciously political, I don't even know myself anymore. That is about to change. I promise you. I clearly see that *what* we deliver and *how* we deliver it is constantly being behaviorally communicated by every single person in our company."

"Samantha, here's what I'd like you to do," said Brandon. "We're going to have a management retreat in about a week. I'll be facilitating it. Between now and then, I want you to create a list of what you believe you can contribute in the way of training and coaching to help your people strengthen your Brand. Give us a conceptual outline of what the programs would look like and what resources you would need."

"Outstanding. Do you want a copy of my report before the retreat?"

"No, just bring your report with you along with copies for everyone."

"Joe," Samantha said, "is there anything that you want from me before the retreat?" The excitement in her voice said that she was truly on board.

"I'm fine with what Brandon asked for. This has been a great meeting. I look forward to hearing what you have to say at our retreat. We'll get out of your hair now. Thanks again for your input. And I appreciate your candor."

Two warm handshakes later, Joe and Brandon left her office. Samantha turned, walked slowly to her desk, sat down, leaned back in her chair, closed her eyes, and took a long, measured deep breath. *Talk about a potentially career-changing meeting. Holy shit. This could be it.*

A little, well-placed contrition never hurt. She congratulated herself on her well-delivered, spontaneous performance. Her political instincts served her well once again. Now it was time to think and strategize.

Who is this Brandon Strong character? During her years in the Fortune 500 world, she had seen hundreds of consultants come and go. She had never heard of him. Neither Joe nor Brandon ever mentioned Brandon's connection to a consulting organization; he never offered her his business card. *Where has he been? What has he done? Despite his apparent lack of stature, however, Brandon certainly appeared to know his stuff. And it was obvious that Joe had confidence in him.*

It seemed all but certain that Brandon's definition of their Brand would soon become one of the cornerstones of their culture. She needed to make sure that her training initiatives were seen as essential in shaping that new culture.

She was still the new kid on the block, and she would need allies at the retreat. Who could she get to align with her?

Mark Selisman? No way. He was a resource hog; if there was an extra dime to spend on anything, Mark wanted it. Besides, he was all about message, not the subtleties of communication.

Ben Counter? Another no. He wanted everything quantified and measured from the get-go. That would be difficult to impossible, at least at the onset of her programs.

Erika Opensource? A question mark. She seemed totally focused on her own area and didn't seem interested in much of anything else. What would it take to win her over?

Manny Factura? Maybe. Manny would have to see her programs as directly benefiting his people in their day-to-day work. She could make that happen, but could she convince Manny quickly enough?

Desi Concepcion? Yes. Desi's creative perspective would help him see how better interpersonal skills would translate to enhanced customer experiences and a stronger Brand. And that would eventually translate into more design resources for Desi.

Joe Fenington? Joe was philosophically already there. With one or two other executives supporting her training initiatives, he would definitely come through with the needed resources.

So much for power and politics. Samantha's thoughts now turned to the reason she came to Kitchen Sculpture. *She really did want to make a difference. She believed in the good that she could bring to people by giving them more effective interpersonal skills. Tying her programs to improving their Brand made perfect sense. If political guile was required to achieve her goals, so be it.* In her mind the ends justified the means.

Samantha never considered the fact that when it came to political skills, Brandon was three steps ahead of her.

Chapter 11

Premature Elation

As Joe and Brandon headed back to Joe's office, Joe walked with a spring in his step and a smile on his face.

"That," said Joe, "was a breath of fresh air."

"Perhaps."

"Perhaps? Are you kidding me? I just heard my Vice President of Human Resources, a former Fortune 500 senior executive, apologize for being less than creative and not aggressive enough in her own area of responsibility. I heard her commit to being better. I heard her agree with your definition of our Brand and pledge to make it part of her training platform. What in the world did you hear that makes all that sound like 'perhaps'?"

"I heard the same things you did. But I'm also considering the source. I heard them from an experienced, politically savvy corporate executive who knows how to move her agenda through the provincial pits of prevention associated with significant change. She knows when to push, when to sit back, when and how to be contrite—like today. Joe, when it comes to political manipulation, Samantha could eat you alive and digest your carcass before you realized your heart stopped. She's not only good; she also knows that she's better at it than anyone else in your organization." Brandon spoke with the cynicism of experience. His words crashed down on Joe like a bucket of ice-cold water poured on a groggy boxer. "On the other hand, I also think that Samantha is sincere in her beliefs about the benefits of her programs. And I believe that what she's recommending can have a monumental effect on your ability to strengthen your Brand."

"If that's true, what's the difference whether or not she's good at corporate politics? She's working to help or company in ways that we need and that are consistent with strengthening our Brand."

"I agree, up to a point. The unanswered question for me is, what happens if there comes a point where her programs somehow don't make the kind of difference or produce the level of benefit that she projects? If that were to happen, does her desire for power override her interest in what's best for the company? At this point we don't know. That's why I'm saying—perhaps."

"Are you telling me she can't be trusted?"

"I'm saying I don't know yet. I think time and circumstances will give you a better picture than you have right this minute. I suggest that you give her enough rope to do her job, but not so much that she can get out of control before anyone finds out. Ben Counter can be a big help in that area—not subversively, mind you, just by having the kinds of measured accountability in place that you would want for any major new program."

"And I thought we just had a great meeting," said Joe, feeling somewhat crestfallen. "Remind me never to ask you again."

"Joe, it's not bad. Just be appropriately cautious. Samantha has been here, what, about a year? And in that year she's had to focus on integrating the human resource requirements associated with your acquisitions. She's probably having a few 'out of the frying pan into the fire' thoughts about why she came here in the first place. Right about now I think she's chomping at the bit to get some meaningful training programs going. That's a good thing."

"OK, so what's next?" said Joe. "Are we ready for our retreat?"

"We are. Here's what I'm thinking. Today is Wednesday, the sixth. I think we should hold a two-day, off-site retreat on Saturday and Sunday of next week. That would be the sixteenth and seventeenth. That will give everyone, you included, a chance to digest what's happened so far. As to the weekend, I know it's asking a lot ..."

"You don't have to justify the weekend time slot. Our people know from experience that mid-week retreats don't have the same energy as those we've had on weekends. And they all have understanding families. So that sounds good. There's a quiet hotel within an hour's drive of here. We've used it before. I'll get Alice on it first thing tomorrow."

"Joe, I hope you know that this could be a life-changing experience."

"Brandon, after all the blind faith I've placed in you and this whole crazy ride we're on—it better be—or I'm going to spend the next year on some shrink's couch."

Chapter 12
A Little Panic

On Wednesday the 13th at 5:00 p.m., Mark Selisman and Sharon, his assistant, huddled in Mark's office.

"The retreat is this weekend. What have you got for me?" asked Mark. His usual intensity was up a notch.

"Well," said Sharon, her voice just above a whisper, "somewhere between very little and nothing."

Mark blanched. "How can that be?"

"I checked all my sources," said Sharon, doing her best imitation of a CIA agent tracking a wanted terrorist.

"And?"

"And nothing. This Brandon Strong guy has no address, no driver's license, no social security number, and no credit cards. I checked utility records; I did a criminal background check. Nothing. I Googled him up, down, and sideways. I'm telling you, he doesn't exist."

"He must be using an alias," said Mark. *But why?* he asked himself. *What does he have to hide? And Joe must be in on the identity thing as well. He would never retain someone he didn't know anything about. Are they after me? Calm down, big guy. He's talking to every executive.*

"What did you learn about what Brandon is saying to people?"

"Well, from what I could gather from my sources, he's talking to everyone about the same thing—our Brand. He's asking them what they think it is and then telling them his definition. He and Joe have met with everyone on the executive team. It all sounds pretty boring, if you ask me."

"Did my name come up in any of those meetings?"

"A few times, from what I was told, but not in a threatening way, from what I was told. Do you want me to try to find out more?"

Mark thought for a moment. *Well, it doesn't sound like anyone is questioning my performance, not that there's any reason to. This sounds too straightforward. There's got to be more to it. But what? And why? I hate level playing fields. I like to have an edge. I'll just have to figure out Brandon's game at the retreat. Damn.*

"No, Sharon. I think we're fine. You did a good job. Thanks for your help."

"You're welcome, Mark. If there's anything else …"

"Yes, I'll let you know."

OK Mr. Brandon Strong, highly recommended Brand consultant, no one is going to take away one inch of my turf. Game on.

The Retreat

Chapter 13

Introduction To Awareness

The hotel's pastoral ambience could not calm the collective anxiety that permeated the room. Each participant experienced his or her own versions of the awkwardness one so often feels when invited to an important event but is not sure what to wear. Seeing one another and sensing the collective angst didn't help. Greetings and salutations ended in question marks: "Good morning?"; "Good to see you?"; "Beautiful day?"; and "You look great?"

Brandon stood in stark contrast to everyone else; he was posed and poised at the head of a large, U-shaped table, looking as relaxed as if he had just come from a spa after a two-hour massage. Joe stood next to him, smiling at everyone, valiantly trying to appear relaxed. He and Brandon had earlier agreed that Joe would be a participant along with everyone else. Brandon would lead the retreat, solo.

If the energy in the room could speak it would have said, *Who in the hell is this guy? Why has he had such a profound effect on everyone? He's either the best con man ever, or some kind of prophet. He seems to have so eloquently relayed a profound, simple truth that no one had even thought of before.*

The week of preparation and introspection had worked just as Brandon had envisioned. Healthy curiosity mixed with a tinge of fear of the unknown had sharpened the senses and made for creative possibilities. Brandon stood silently, as the participants continued to talk to one another. Gradually, the energy in the room shifted from the discomfort of uncertainty to the electric vibrations of adventure. *We've reached that pivotal moment,* Brandon thought. *They're ready to begin.*

Chapter 14
Candor And Conflict

"Good morning, everyone," Brandon began.

"Good morning," came the collective reply.

"We all sort of know why we're here," said Brandon, "but let me explicitly set forth our objectives." On a large screen he brought up a PowerPoint slide that read:

- *Our Brand is a widely held set of beliefs and expectations about what we deliver and how we deliver it, validated by customers' experiences.*

- By the end of our retreat we will collectively adopt this new definition of our Brand, for ourselves individually and for our organization as a whole. And we will have articulated and answered the important critical questions essential in getting to that place.

- In subscribing to this new definition, we will fully understand the implications of that definition and the roles we as leaders must play in moving our culture to that place.

"As you all know, Joe and I spoke with each of you individually. During those discussions, I asked you to tell me your definition of your Brand. Let's begin by having all of us see what everyone had to say." With that, Brandon passed out a document that summarized each person's definition of Kitchen Sculpture's Brand:

Mark Selisman: *Our Brand is our public identity. It's what separates us and differentiates us from our competitors. It's the story of our products' superiority, compressed into compelling messages that people remember. It presents our products in a way that makes people want to buy them. It's a picture, it's a promise, and it's a perceived experience that we put in people's minds through the power of our advertising, marketing, and public relations presence.*

Manny Factura: *Our Brand is all the stuff that the people in marketing say it is in all of our advertising. It's the great design of our products, their features and functionality, dependability, uniqueness, and sculptural nature.*

Ben Counter: *Our Brand is an asset. Its three main components are name recognition, name attractiveness, and name retention. Its purpose is to bring in revenue. Its cost is all the money we spend to create it, even though it doesn't show up that way on our balance sheet. It appreciates in value when we hit the mark with our message and our programs and people buy more of our products than we projected. It depreciates when we do things to tarnish it; or when we send messages that drive people away from us rather than toward us. It diminishes in value when our competitors send more compelling messages than ours, or when people get tired of our products and stop buying them, or when we don't maintain a consistent enough message for people to remember us.*

Desi Concepcion: *Our Brand is the total feeling that people get when they see our products, use our products, and react to their experience of our products. It's a visceral thing, not an advertising message. Marketing and advertising is just the wrapping. The real deal is inside the box—our products and what they deliver. Different emotions come into play when people experience our products. They get a sensual pleasure from using them because our products don't just perform, they interact with their owners; customers get a tactile pleasure from simply touching and feeling the sculptural artistry in our products; and they get a sense of pride when they show off the products to their friends because our products are seen as status symbols. When we deliver the experience I just described, our Brand is strong. When we don't, our Brand weakens.*

Erika Opensource: *Our Brand is about connection. I'm talking about how people become loyal to us, to our products, how they want to engage with us and tell us what they like and don't like, how they come to trust us, how they want to be able to tell us what new features they want, what new products they want, how they like or don't like how it is to do business with us, how they want to have a dialogue with us and not just have advertising messages shoved down their throats. Connection, dude.*

Samantha Persons: *I think our Brand is all the things that the marketing and advertising world say about what a Brand is. A whole lot of awareness attributes that focus on name recognition and reputation. I strongly believe, however, that our Brand is also enhanced by our people's interpersonal skills, their ability to listen effectively to our customers, to communicate effectively, and to exhibit compassion. All of these qualities directly affect customers' attitudes about our company. They comprise the human component of our Brand. And of course, if we don't do those things well, our Brand can be damaged.*

"Now," said Brandon, "I'm going to show you my synthesized version of what I got from your definitions." With that he displayed another Power Point slide:

Our Brand is:

- Message power: the appeal and reach of our image; the promise of the value we represent; the creation of expectations that satisfy needs and wants; and our demonstrated ability to deliver on all of it.

- Product quality, uniqueness, functionality.

- An asset made up of name recognition, attractiveness, and retention—with fluctuating, performance-based measurable value.

- Emotional connection to our products from the tactile experience of interacting with them.

- Connection—the building of trust and conversation between our customers and us, culminating in a collaborative relationship.
- The quality of our interaction with our customers, defined by our ability to listen, to understand, and to display sensitivity to our customers' needs and desires.

"What this list shows me," said Brandon, "is that, collectively, you have identified many, but not all, of the pieces touched on by my definition of your Brand. Anyone want to comment on that?" He looked at each person sitting around the table.

No one uttered a sound.

Finally Joe spoke. "I've never seen this group so quiet. You guys usually don't even have to be asked. Why so bashful?" Still no response. "Never mind. I'll go first. I think everything we're looking at talks to our Brand. And I can also see that the kind of things that Brandon talked about in our individual one-on-one meetings that are not shown here are also parts of our Brand. I'm still not a hundred percent convinced that the definition of our Brand is quite as extensive as Brandon thinks it is, but I'm willing to be persuaded. What I'm not quite sure of is how being more inclusive in our definition translates into better performance and results."

Joe's little speech broke the ice, making it easier for the others to say what they thought, but had feared saying—or at least saying it first.

"Exactly," said Mark.

"Kiss ass," said Manny before Mark could continue. He said it with a hangdog grin that triggered relaxed laughter from everyone.

Engagement had begun.

Mark continued. "I think that too broad a definition of our Brand could actually cause us to misuse some of our resources and divert our attention away from building and strengthening our Brand. Don't you agree, Joe?"

Without warning, Desi pounced. "Are you trying to end this meeting before it begins? What was that bullshit, some kind of trial close to stifle open discussion? We didn't come here to listen to you pontificate."

Joe started to jump in, but Brandon put his hand on Joe's arm and stopped him.

"Shh. Allow me," he whispered.

"Actually, Desi," said Brandon, "there might be some merit in what Mark is saying. It depends not only on what you use as your definition of your Brand, but also on how that definition comes to life in the day-to-day activities of your people. However, it seems like there's more on your mind than Mark's comment. Care to share?"

"Sure, what the hell. I was going to wait until later, but I might as well get it out of my system now. No point in letting it keep boiling inside me." He swallowed and took a long, slow, deep breath. "You all know that I feel our products are living, breathing, functional, works of art. OK, so then we acquire three small companies that have knocked off some of our products by making design changes that convert them from art to somewhat attractive, pedestrian kitchen appliances and have been selling them to a whole different customer niche at much lower prices. I get it. I understand Joe's argument that if someone is going to knock us off, it ought to be us. But here's where we part company. All of you guys are approaching this by looking at taking our existing products and dumbing down the design to save tooling and production costs. So what we end up with is inferior design at a lower price. I know we can do better. If you would just give me the budget dollars to hire some additional design resources we could design lower-price products with a clean-sheet-of-paper approach. We would absolutely kick some ass in the mid-price category."

Manny jumped in. "But Desi, you and I argue all the time about design complexity. And we always get to a compromise that satisfies your artistic sense and still allows us to make the products at prices just below the stratosphere so there are a few people left on the planet who can afford them. So what's the difference between that and going further and, like you said, dumbing them down to an even lower price? Seems to me it's cheaper to do that than start with a clean sheet of paper. And I think that it also shortens our design cycle so we can come out with products faster. I don't get why you're so upset, Desi."

Mark saw his chance. "He's just pissed because he screwed up his last mid-price blender design and it's cracking for no reason. And he's looking to blame someone else for his mistake."

Desi's laser stare could have burned holes through lead. But before he could find words, Samantha dove in headfirst. "OK, gentlemen. Tempers are getting a little testy. It seems to me that there are some issues that have been smoldering for quite some time."

"Really?" said Desi, waving his arms with Shakespearian flair. "Your perceptions are astounding."

Samantha didn't flinch. "Seriously, I think that we all need to get to the core of what's really bothering both of you if we're going to get past this and make some progress here."

A new dynamic was taking shape. Samantha stepped into the middle of an emotional storm, and no one questioned her claim on the role of mediator. She was careful to cast the briefest of sideways glances at Joe to take a quick reading on his attitude. He seemed fine, even relieved, that he was not playing the role. So far, so good, she thought.

Desi slowly stood up, stared at Mark, then Manny; his eyes came to rest on Joe. "Joe, I think you know what's bothering me. No, not bothering me, eating my guts out. But we might as well get it on the table once and for all, for everyone to see." Desi didn't raise his voice, but his words hit the air like machine-gun bullets strafing anyone in their path.

"Please go on," said Joe. "I agree, let's get it on the table."

Desi remained standing as he began. "As we all know, when we acquired the companies in the mid-price channel, we did it to speed our entry into that market segment while still seemingly offering the cache of the Kitchen Sculpture name. All the companies, then and now, who are knocking us off are doing so by trying to copy the overall look and feel of our products, but they're leaving out all the artistic elements that translate into higher manufacturing costs."

Mark found it impossible to sit quietly. Suddenly his mouth leaped ahead of his brain. "Desi, is there a point here? We already know this stuff. We're wasting valuable time."

"Shut up. Don't interrupt me. You can speak when I'm finished. You just can't handle not being the center of the universe for more than five minutes." Desi was on the verge of one of his ballistic meltdowns.

The air in the room surged from tense to high voltage. Eyes darted between Mark and Desi.

Samantha jumped in before Joe could speak. She was relishing her emerging mediator role. "Gentleman, please. Desi has a point that I think we all need to observe over the next two days—don't interrupt the speaker. We'll get a lot further if we can all do that. Sorry Mark, I'm not trying to single you out, it's just that you—"

"I know, I know," said Mark. "Sorry." Even feigned contrition was not Mark's strong suit. But he silently congratulated himself for his effort. *Just wait, big guy. Your chance is coming. Give Desi a little more rope. The gallows are within sight.*

Desi collected himself and continued. "As I was saying"—and a roll of his eyes elicited relieved laughter and lightened the air just a bit— "everyone is chasing us, copying our designs. When we do the same thing, we're not bringing anything new to the party. It's just us behaving exactly like our competitors. We're boring. We have the ability to be sooo much better than that. If we had just one designer devoted to our mid-price line, start with a fresh perspective, work with Manny's manufacturing engineers to define our manufacturing constraints, and design some new mid-price products that are truly original, I believe we could dominate that segment. But we must allocate the appropriate resources."

Desi was on a roll. It sounded compelling to several in the room—but not to everyone.

Mark started. "Desi, you said we were boring. I don't see it that way at all. The market we're introducing our products to has never seen anything like them before. It's all brand-new to them. That doesn't sound boring to me. In addition, most of the people in that market don't have anything approaching your taste level and design sense. Hell, a lot of people who buy our mainstream products don't get what you're trying to convey. They just know that their friends have them and they better get one too in order to keep up. It's a status thing, not a taste thing. So what's wrong with knocking off our existing designs? It's a whole lot faster, and cheaper. Or have you lost sight of our sales and profit goals?"

The last question was meant to start a confrontation. It almost worked. Manny stopped it.

"Don't go gettin' snippy on us, Mr. Superstar. You're no one to talk. Hell, if it was up to you, our marketing budget would make the cost of the war in Iraq look like petty cash."

Erika couldn't hold it in. "Amen to that, dude."

The gloves were coming off. Joe was visibly disturbed, not by the content but by the tone of the conversation; personal attacks were in stark contrast to their core values. His team was frayed at the edges, maybe worse. *How did I not see this before? Did the acquisitions bring this on? Were the pressures of expansion and integration more than they could handle? Or were the problems there before, and the acquisitions just put them in the spotlight?*

On the defensive, Mark took over. "OK, so because a few uninformed people don't understand what it takes to run an effective marketing and sales organization, that means we abandon the need to design the most profitable mid-price products? Is that what you guys are trying to say?"

"Chill, dude. No one said that." Erika was in character.

"Well, that's the implication I heard," said Mark.

"Then get your system checked. Make sure your ears are connected to your brain." Erika had officially decided to abandon civility. Consciously or not, she had also moved collective emotions closer to meltdown.

Joe was now beside himself. At Brandon's insistence, he hadn't spoken yet, but he just couldn't let this attack-fest continue. Looking at Brandon, he saw only calmness in his face and body language. What did Brandon know that he didn't? *All right, I'll keep silent for now, but at the next sign of trouble all bets are off.*

Desi got back to his position. "No, Mark, I haven't lost sight of our need to sell products and make money. But at what long-term cost to our reputation, and, as Brandon defines it, our Brand? For the past year I've been hit with impossible demands to rush new mid-price products to market before we've had a chance to properly check our work on design modifications. I haven't had a good night's sleep since our recall. I know it was my design. I also know we took all kinds of shortcuts with our environmental stress tests in order to get the damn thing out so Mark could fulfill his promises to customers—promises he made without checking with Manny or me before he opened his big mouth. So, Marky boy, in order to make you look good, I created a piece of crap—and now we're all paying for it."

Silence fell. Everyone stared at their own private spot, somewhere on the table in front of them, afraid to even make eye contact with anyone.

Joe leaned over and, behind his hand, whispered to Brandon, "For God's sakes, man, aren't you going to say something?"

"Yes, yes I am," he whispered back as he carefully surveyed the room and then announced, "Well now, I think this is a good time to take a short break. Let's be back in fifteen minutes."

Chapter 15

A Much Needed Breather

Brandon and Joe remained seated as they observed the nervous stampede through the door and into the private lobby. The worry lines etched across his forehead made Joe appear ten years older. "This is not going well, not well at all," he said, to no one in particular, although Brandon was the only other person in the room. "How can you sit there so calmly? I'm seeing my team disintegrate into a dysfunctional pile of poop as you just calmly watch. I thought you were supposed to moderate and motivate and move our people toward embracing a new definition of our Brand. Instead, they're launching personal attacks against one another that have nothing to do with our Brand. I'm witnessing a shocking disregard for our Core Values. What the hell are you doing?" Joe's agitation grew with each word out of his mouth.

"Hmm," said Brandon, his hand slowly stroking his chin. "Let me tell you something, my friend. First of all, the pent-up anger, the personal attacks, and the disregard for your Values—they all have a great deal to do with your Brand. They directly impact what you deliver and how you deliver it. Were you so focused on peoples' emotions that you didn't hear the message? Mark made promises that strained your organization's capacity to deliver on. He never bothered to coordinate with his colleagues. Desi, reacting emotionally to a conflicted mix of meeting sales goals while ignoring quality standards, designed, in his words, 'a piece of crap.' What does that say about your Brand? And Desi's personal standards were violated. I can tell you that from the perspective of a creative soul like Desi's, he feels like he was raped. As to your company's Values? Right now, some of those Values are just empty words. If your people are ignoring them, you need to pay attention, because at this moment, they are not your Values. The way people are actually behaving represents your Values. Don't be deluded by warm words on a wall plaque."

As Brandon spoke, Joe's body language shifted from attack to surrender; his face morphed from snarl to scolded puppy. "Brandon, I'm just too close to the situation, too emotionally involved to get above the tree line and see what's going on. What do we do? What do I do now?"

"Joe, you're right to be concerned. This is serious. Try to relax, as much as you can. Become a sponge. Soak up the information that's being given to us. It's golden."

"But these personal attacks can't possibly be doing anybody any good. We should stop them as soon as we resume. I'm going to step in and do that."

"Not just yet," said Brandon. "People have been holding their feelings in for a long time. What you don't know is how much backstabbing and political maneuvering has been going on every day, and for how long. We need to get this stuff out in the open before we snuff it. And it also gives people a chance to empty their tanks, get it out of their systems so they can be more open to new input. I'll know when to stop it. Trust me."

"OK," said Joe, with a resigned tone. "I'll leave it up to you. I need to go make a phone call. I'll see you back here in a few."

As Joe headed out the door, Brandon sat back and reflected for a moment. *Wow,* he thought. *This is going well. Events are moving forward faster than I expected. And sometimes, even though it's not productive, it's fun to sit back and watch a good fight.*

Chapter 16
A Break And A Breakthrough

As Brandon exited the meeting room and entered their private lobby, he noticed that the participants had each found the people with whom they wanted to debrief. Manny, Erika, and Desi were quietly talking in one corner. Samantha and Ben had their heads together in another. Mark was slowly pacing up and down the length of the room, but as soon as he saw Brandon, he quickly strode over.

"Brandon, may I have a word with you?"

"Of course, Mark."

"I have to tell you that I resent Desi's remarks. First of all, he's an emotional prima donna. Second, he doesn't have a clue about what we're dealing with in the mid-price market. Third, all he's interested in is proving to the world that he's the Michelangelo of appliance design."

"So you think this is about Desi's need for recognition and not about your Brand?"

"You bet your ass that's what I think."

Brandon stared intently into Mark's eyes as he spoke. "Mark, what is the purpose of this conversation? What do you want to happen as a result of us talking?" He held up his hand as Mark began to respond.

"And before you answer, I'm going to tell you what it feels like to me. It feels like you're lobbying for my approval of your point of view. And with that approval comes leverage—and power. Power over Desi. Am I wrong?"

No words were needed. Mark's "hand in the cookie jar" expression said it all. His feeble attempt to appear offended only made matters worse. Brandon started to laugh, but stifled it so as not to alert the others in the lobby. "Mark," he said softly, "you're a terrible actor. But it's OK."

Mark reacted quickly. If feigned, righteous indignation didn't work, maybe blatant honesty might. "So what if my motive is exactly what you said it is? What's wrong with that? I'm trying to persuade you to see my position, agree with it, and try to get Desi to act sensibly. You do that, and get Joe on board, then I guarantee you, we sell more products, make more money, and everyone is happy. Is that a problem?"

"Wow," said Brandon, "two trial closes in two sentences. You're a ballsy salesman Mark. I like your style—almost. First of all, I think we've agreed that your motive is what I said it was—to gain my support for your point of view over Desi's. As to whether or not that's a problem— yes, it's a big problem, and here's why. We're talking behind Desi's back instead of showing him the respect that he and your organization deserves. Now I know that that is contrary to your core values. There is absolutely no respect or integrity in what you just did. Even if I believed in the doctrine of the ends justifying the means, and I don't, this situation doesn't rise to that level."

"That all sounds very noble, Brandon, but aren't you being just a tad naive here? I mean, conversations are had and deals like this are made all day long in business and in government. Congress, for example."

"Are you're telling me that you want to use Congress—an institution with an approval rating lower than al Qaida's—as your standard of quality? Are you serious? I'm not naive. I'm talking about integrity.

"But the integrity issue is just one of my problems, Mark. Here's another one. With your approach, you make Desi your adversary, not your teammate. Rather than collaborating, you're competing. New ideas that might arise from exploring your differences aren't possible. Conflict can be the cradle of creativity. But you don't want to rock that cradle, you just want an internal dogfight. In the end it might feel like someone wins and someone loses, but the reality is that everyone loses: the company, your customers, and, ironically, the people who think they've won."

Mark stood silently, but this time his silence was genuine. His wheels were not turning; he wasn't framing his response or planning his next move. He was actually processing Brandon's words.

Brandon glanced up and saw Joe returning. The others were finishing their conversations and were headed back toward the meeting room.

"We can pick this up later if you like," said Brandon.

"Uh, yes. Yes, we can. I'd like that," said Mark, and he turned to head back with the others.

Good break, thought Brandon. *Damn good break.*

Chapter 17

The Trials Of Transition

Though some of the tension was diffused during the break, a thin cloud of nervousness still hung in the air. Now that Brandon knew where and with whom the hot-button issues lay, he decided to begin on a calmer note.

"Ben," he began. "You haven't said a word yet. Let's start with you." A silent, collective sigh of relief spread throughout the room. Normal breathing resumed.

Brandon continued addressing Ben. "When you gave me your definition of your Brand and I gave you mine, I asked you to think about what you would do as a player, rather than as a scorekeeper, to support your new Brand definition. What have you come up with?"

"Well," said Ben. "I had a couple of meetings with my managers, explained the new definition, and we brainstormed about how we might become an integral part of our Brand. So far, we've landed on three areas. *One: we can pose more relevant questions relating to our Brand when we prepare our monthly performance reports. Two: we can better analyze our product sales by customer, ferret out dealers whose overall performance has remained flat, and give that information to Mark so he, in turn, can reach out to our customers to help them improve their sales where we see opportunities; and three, we can get much closer to and be more proactive with our customers through our credit department."*

"Any comments?" Brandon asked the group.

Mark's territorial instincts set off an alarm inside his head. "What exactly are you thinking of having our credit people doing with our customers?"

"Glad you asked," said Ben. "Our approach to credit management has been to do our credit checking at the time we get a new customer. Once we determine that the new customer is creditworthy, we set up their account, establish their credit limit, and then leave them alone as long as they pay their bills on time. When customers exceed their credit limits, our system sets off alerts. Once an alert pops up, we examine the customer's buying trends and their payment history. We contact them, get current financial information, determine if we need to adjust their credit limit, secure their account with liens on their assets, file UCC1s, et cetera. The thing is, we get involved only when results stray outside our performance parameters. If things remain normal, as they do for the majority of our customers, we don't get involved in our customers' business. In other words, we've been operating on the principle of management by exception.

"But here's the thing." Ben paused for a brief moment to craft his next statement. "Our credit people have been conditioned to see zero change as a reason to do nothing. But, if you think about it, no change means no growth. We don't know if the customer's entire business is static or if they just aren't selling more of our products. So 'no change' might be an opportunity for us to come up with some creative campaigns to help our customers increase their sales of KS products. At the least, it's an opportunity for us to show an interest in them and have some meaningful dialogue."

"Who do you mean by 'us'?" Mark challenged.

"I mean you and your team, Mark." Ben's tone, which had been reasoned and thoughtful, shifted at Mark's transparent territorialism. Others noticed this shift, especially Joe. "I said that we would provide you with information," he continued, clearly displaying irritation. "I never said or implied that my people would directly contact our customers. Did you not hear me?" His words, spoken through clenched teeth, sharpened Ben's message. Mark knew he was headed toward the crosshairs of one of Ben's guided missiles.

"Hold on," said Mark. "I'm just trying to clarify our respective actions. This is new to us. We're all feeling our way. At least I am. And Ben—and everyone else, for that matter"— he turned to the room at large—"you need to know, if you don't already, that my department has reporting systems in place to track our dealers' sales. We look at monthly, quarterly, and year-to-date sales. We compare those results to the same periods for the previous three years. And we compare our actual results to our sales forecasts. We track by demographic group, by model, and by color to determine changing tastes. We track in ways that you guys can't imagine," he continued, getting a little testy. "So Ben, if you think that you've come up with a way to measure sales growth, or the absence of growth, that we're not already doing, I don't think so. It's great that you and your people are thinking outside of *your* box. But I don't believe your time will be well spent giving me information that we already have."

"You're right, Mark, and I apologize for not being more clear," Ben said. "Yet I still think the information we can provide might open some new opportunities. You look at sales. We look at financial stability. If a customer has flat sales, you try to create marketing programs to increase their sales. We pay for those programs out of our marketing budget. As part of that process you arm-wrestle with me and the other vice presidents to get as big a budget allocation as you can to fund your activities. And because you're so good at making your case, you're considered a resource hog and not a team player."

Silent nods of agreement resounded throughout the room. Joe and Brandon felt the energy. Mark did not. As was typically the case when it came to objective analysis, Ben was right on target. Mark started to rebut, but Ben cut him off.

"Let me finish my point," he said, holding up a hand. "We don't attempt to design marketing incentive programs. But in analyzing a given customer's financial stability, our credit people are able to create additional working capital for our credit-worthy customers by offering them extended terms, or in special cases, inventory on consignment. They, in turn, can use the additional capital we create for them to help them pay for sales promotions programs that your marketing team and theirs can develop together. That way, we become better true partners in our customers' success, not simply arms-length vendors. I believe that what I just suggested addresses both the *what* and the *how* in our Brand."

"Bean for president," Manny shouted.

"You are freakin' hot, dude," Erika chimed in.

"Merlin the munificent has muttered," Desi added, complete with hand flourishes.

Ben's ear-to-ear grin flashed as he relished his delicious moment of triumph; but it quickly retreated behind his chief-financial-officer sternness. "Not so fast with the praise," he cautioned. "The main responsibility falls on Mark's team. I didn't mean this to sound like we're just going to throw money at our dealers. Once we determine how much additional working capital we can create, it will fall on Mark to develop marketing promotions that allow us to measure our return on investment based on increases in sales and profits directly attributable to these promotions. The measurement architecture must be built into the programs from the start, not based on loosey-goosey assumptions created after the fact. But we're getting ahead of ourselves. At this point it's just an idea."

"And a damn good one," said Mark. All eyes swung to Mark. *What did he say? Did he actually praise someone else's marketing idea? Had there been a full moon last night?* "C'mon people, don't everyone look at me like I'm nuts. It's a good idea. OK, so I don't say that very often."

"How about I'm writing this down as a first," said Manny.

"This," Brandon whispered as he leaned over to Joe, "is headed in the right direction."

Joe quietly nodded in agreement. And for the first time since the retreat began, the corners of his mouth turned slightly upward, and a smile was born.

"Ben, how about the two of us meet after the retreat and talk your idea through, really flesh it out and see how we can implement it," said Mark.

"Sounds good. I look forward to it," Ben replied. A tone of collegiality had crept into Mark and Ben's exchange. It was in stark contrast to the barely civil, often heated arm wrestling that had become their norm.

Brandon stood and slowly took a few steps back and forth as he spoke. "Have you all seen what has transpired during this exchange? Have you felt the energy in the room shift? Have you seen the kind of progress we've made in the last ten minutes compared to the previous thirty?"

"It's all about Mark giving someone besides himself a compliment," said Manny. "I swear I felt the earth move."

The group burst out in laughter, which Brandon interrupted before Mark could. "Actually, Manny, you're closer to the truth than you might think. Anyone else?"

Samantha saw her moment. "Yes; we began to attack the issue rather than each other. We got passionate, not angry. It's a great illustration of what can happen when people become effective communicators."

"All kidding aside," said Manny, "it was easy to feel the difference, and Samantha described it perfectly. Not to brag or anything, but it's the way I try to have my people talk to each other all the time. They don't always do it, but when they do, we get a lot more done, and we get it done faster."

"I agree," said Ben. "And I definitely felt a shift in the tone of Mark's and my conversation. Did you feel it, Mark?"

"Yes I did," he said. "Not so much while we were talking as I did afterward. That's when it hit me. I guess I'm so used to the old street-fight way that it seems normal. Attacking the issue, like you said, Samantha, definitely feels better. I guess I need to work on that. But I'm not really sure of how to do that without giving up my point of view, and I'm sure as hell not willing to do that."

"Don't worry about that right now," said Samantha. "There are some really good techniques I can teach you. Assaulting the issue without surrendering your point of view is so doable you'll wonder how you ever approached situations differently. In the meantime, just focus on how good it felt a few minutes ago when you had that experience."

"I want to add something," said Joe. "I've kept quieter than usual because I really wanted to focus on hearing you guys and not just listening to myself talk. What I heard at the end of the conversation between Mark and Ben, though, is a good illustration of the difference between real teamwork and the creeping silo behavior that I believe we've all been experiencing over the last year. I don't know if we can properly address that issue at this retreat as part of our agenda, or if we need to address it in some other way. I'm willing to leave that up to Brandon. But either way, we need to address it, and soon. And Mark, Ben—I want to commend you both for the way you came together around an idea. We need more of that."

"Anyone else," said Brandon, looking first at Desi, then Erika.

"I'm good," said Erika.

"So am I," added Desi.

"Let me quickly comment about what Joe just said," said Brandon. "Silos can cripple your Brand. They are toxic. They inhibit the kind of teamwork needed to deliver the best of who you are. Oftentimes, people who operate in silo environments don't see themselves or their cultures in that way. They don't see the subversive nature of the structures they inhabit. I'd like you all to think about how you share information between functional areas of your company, how you work together, or not, as a team, how those things affect the quality of your decisions, and how all of that impacts the *what* and the *how* of your Brand. And finally"— Brandon's gaze made contact with each and every one of the group— "think about whether or not you live in a silo culture. And I promise, Joe, we will definitely address silos during our time together. Anyone want to comment?"

Dead silence.

"OK, then, we'll move along," said Brandon.

Despite Brandon's last comments, the mood in the room had turned positive. They had made a huge leap after their morning break. At least most of them had.

Chapter 18

Conspiracy Dressed As Collaboration

When Manny, Desi, and Erika powwowed during the break, the target of their conversation had been Mark. Manny's problems with Mark boiled down to one issue—collaboration. Mark almost never talked to him in advance about production scheduling before allowing his salespeople to make special commitments to customers, nor did he consult with him about deadlines for trade shows and promotional events. Manny's conclusion: Mark's arrogance and need for control made teamwork impossible.

Desi had repeatedly fought with Mark over their approach to the design of their newly acquired mid-price products. What divided them was Mark's insistence on speed versus Desi's desire for uniqueness, which required a somewhat longer product development process. For Desi, reasoning with Mark was fruitless. Mark listened only to the sound of his own voice. When he believed that he was right—and that was all the time—he dismissed others with an arrogance that could provoke workplace violence. Desi's conclusion: Mark's arrogant attitude and close-minded view of the company's needs made teamwork impossible.

Erika was frustrated because she'd been trying for more than a year to get Mark to use social media to get closer to both their customers and their ultimate consumers. Erika had considerable experience using social-media platforms; she had done extensive research into corporate best practices; she had talked to Ben about the costs of implementing a social media strategy. When she brought the subject up on several occasions at management meetings, she was always told to work it out with Mark. For Erika, that was like talking to the proverbial wall. Mark did not understand social-

media, nor did he want to learn. He defended the status quo because he believed his methods were producing acceptable results. He tied his position to the practical benefits of using "conventional wisdom," not realizing that the true meaning of that term described an inertia that served as an obstacle to being open to new information. Finally Erika gave up. Her conclusion: Mark was not open to any new ideas that were not his own. He was incapable of engaging in true teamwork.

Despite their complaints, they all knew that Mark was intelligent, sometimes brilliant; he worked hard, and sales prospered under his leadership. Because of that, Mark usually had Joe's support. It was hard to argue with results. The only person beside Joe who could effectively go toe-to-toe with Mark was Ben, because Ben was a master at building an evidence-based argument.

But storm clouds were on the horizon. Turnover among the sales staff was higher than it should have been. Salespeople either saw it Mark's way, or they were gone. As the sales force grew, the issue became more problematic and costly. The new sales teams at the mid-price divisions were of an entirely different mind-set than the people at Kitchen Sculpture. Low price was their mantra. Aesthetics, quality, and extraordinary service were not in their DNA. Mark had not bonded with that group. Communications were frequently misinterpreted. Results were not meeting expectations. Tempers were getting short.

The timing seemed right to take a united stand. The three agreed that, during the retreat, they would each bring up their issues with Mark, and they would all be supportive of one another. Mark had to be stopped before his actions threatened the very future of the company, not to mention the quality of their own lives. What better opportunity than in the context of clarifying a new definition of their Brand that focused on "*what* they delivered and *how* they delivered it"! Yes, this was the time to bring Mark down. This was their moment. It didn't occur to them that Brandon might see things differently.

Chapter 19

Light Bulbs For Some

"Desi," said Brandon. "Earlier this morning you talked about the differences you and Mark had over new product design in your new mid-price product line."

"Correct," Desi said, sensing that his moment was near.

"And I asked you during our individual meeting last week to think about those differences in our respective definitions of your Brand and to see how you might change your perception of how you play a more integral role in strengthening your Brand based on the new definition."

"Yes, Brandon. And I've done that. Here's what I think. As I told you and Joe during our meeting, I think advertising and marketing messages are all well and good, but the real communication between our customers and us takes place through our products; more specifically, through our customers interactions with our products. Those experiences create the essence of our Brand. Since our meeting, I have thought more about Brandon's argument that virtually every interaction that anyone in our company has with our customers and each other can impact our Brand. I tend to agree, but I will talk only about the product experience, since that's the way my people and I can affect our Brand.

"I think this new definition impacts our new mid-price product line big time. I'm specifically talking about the 'what' in what we deliver. We acquired some companies that make products designed to somewhat emulate our designs but are sold at much lower prices. That means significant design constraints in order to hit lower price points. And if all we're doing is copying ourselves, I think we're both limiting our appeal and opening the door for competitors. But that's not all." Desi paused dramatically. "There's a greater threat, one that wakes me up in the middle of the night, drenched in a cold sweat."

"Oh my God, I'm dyin' from the suspense," Manny cut in, feeling he needed to lighten the tone. "Please Desi, don't make us wait another minute." Manny knew that Desi would not tolerate that kind of remark from anyone else in the room.

Mark knew it too. "Thank you, Manny," he said. "I wanted to say it, but I knew I'd be killed on the spot."

Light laughter rippled through the room.

"You guys can laugh all you want, and I know you all think I'm overly dramatic, but it's how I feel," Desi said. "And you're just jealous because you don't have the ability to truly express yourselves. OK, where was I?"

"It's the middle of the night and you just woke up trembling in a cold sweat," said Manny.

"As of today," Desi continued, "we have created a unique category for our products and we are virtually the only company in that category. We accomplished it because we were the first to incorporate high-end design to the degree we have in working appliances. And no one has been able to copy us or better us at our level—so far. We occupy a small but highly profitable niche. In addition to design, the other major factor that has enabled us to create our products has been our use of specialty resins—expensive, technically challenging to mold, beautiful-to-look-at resins. That is our current strength and our future vulnerability."

"Why is that a vulnerability?" asked Brandon.

"Because," Desi responded without hesitation, "cheaper, easier to mold, highly durable, attractive materials are coming into the market in the foreseeable future. These new resins are being developed for many other applications in a variety of industries. They're not being developed specifically for our kinds of products. But other companies in our business are as aware of them as we are. They will experiment, and they will develop products that rival ours in design excellence; they will be easier to manufacture in volume, and they will cost a fraction of what it costs to make those kinds of products today."

"Is that a statement of fact, or are those your speculative fears?" asked Mark.

"I sit on several technical committees at three universities. I am close to the chemical and engineering research that is ongoing. The only speculation is about the when; there is no doubt as to the if." He eyeballed Mark directly, then turned to the group. "In my opinion, we have five years, at best, and as little as two years, at worst, before we are staring into the eyes of that reality.

"I believe with all my heart that part of the 'what' of our Brand is artistic, unique design. If we look at our mid-price products in that way, we have both an opportunity and a need to continue delivering that level of distinction. Right now, we're just giving away an entry ticket into the mid-price market to our competitors. All they need to do is wait for the cheaper, easier-to-mold resins, and they'll be able to come pretty damn close to our existing designs with a comparatively low investment threshold of money and talent. But if we seize the opportunity today to develop unique designs for the mid-price market, and don't wait for the new materials to put us in a catch-up mode, we can lead the next wave of innovation without missing a beat," he said with a flourish. "Now, I'm not suggesting that we make and sell everything we develop; we can keep some of our more innovative designs hidden until the next generation of materials becomes a reality. The bottom line is, we must begin today. And no matter how many meltdowns I have"—he turned to Mark again—"I can never get you to listen, Mark. And Joe," he said, turning to look squarely at him, "I haven't gotten your support either. Manny, you're somewhere in the middle. Half the time I don't have a clue where you stand."

Mark could barely contain himself. "Desi, you have never, and I mean never, presented that case to me. Not once. Not in conversations, not in meetings, not in writing. Never."

"Do you have the slightest idea how impossible you are to talk to when you don't agree with someone else's point of view?" Desi snapped back. "I only have to broach the subject of original design and you go rabid with resistance before I can even begin to make a case. We wind up in a shouting match at every meeting, whether it's you and me alone or in a group. I'm sick of it, and I'm sick of your condescending attitude. Do you realize that this is the first time in recent memory that you have allowed me to finish my point before you cut me off?"

"I'm with you on that, dude," said Erika. She was about to launch her own Mark attack, but Brandon stepped in.

"Let's stop right there," he said. "I'd like to pause and have us all look at what is happening here."

"It's obvious what's going on—a dogfight—and it's pretty common around here," Erika piped in.

"Is that what the rest of you see as well?" asked Brandon.

"Pretty much," said Manny.

"I agree," said Ben.

"I see a lack of effective communication skills, skills that are correctible with some training," said Samantha.

Joe chimed in. "I see all those things. And I also see us not living our values. When did mutual respect leave the building? What happened to teamwork? But Brandon, even though this is a serious problem, what does it have to do with our Brand and the reason we're here?"

"Only everything," said Brandon. "We've exposed two issues this morning. One is that you have all created a silo culture. The second is that you're not living what you claim are your core values. The impact of both those things on your Brand is overt and covert. You have incurred measurable costs as well as opportunity costs.

"We've seen an instance of silo mentality costs in your recent product recall. Mark, Desi, and Manny—each of you hunkered down under the mantles of your own authority, responsibility, and blame avoidance, you didn't fully cooperate by being proactive and receptive and consequently, you paid a tangible price. But how will you measure the hidden cost to your Brand? How has your reputation for quality suffered? Do real objects of art mysteriously crack while sitting idly on a shelf? Will people reconsider the premium price you're asking and be more cautious about their buying decisions in the future? I know I may be stretching a point and being a little overly dramatic, but each of you need to ask yourselves how many times over the last year you exhibited silo behavior when you could have dropped your protectionist attitude and cooperated to achieve a greater good?

"As to abandoning your values, I want to hear more experiential examples before I comment. We've still got some time before lunch. I'd like to use that time to talk about what sounds like an important issue, the one that Desi brought up concerning the potentially nightmarish challenges you will face when new resins become a reality. Is everyone in the room surprised, or do some of you already know about this?"

Joe responded immediately. "Desi and I have discussed this issue and his concerns on several occasions. I have to tell all of you that I don't see these changes and competitive challenges in the same life-threatening light as Desi has depicted them. Yes, lower-cost, more easily moldable resins will be developed, and that will give our competitors new opportunities. Yes, our price points will be reduced. However, our ability to innovate and lead the market will be as great or greater than it is today. We will be able to develop unique, proprietary resin compositions that others cannot replicate. Of course, our competitors can ostensibly do the same thing. But we've been at it for so long and have developed such a depth of experience that I believe we have capabilities that will take our competitors many years to replicate. We excel at the complexities of material formulation.

"Let me briefly digress with an example. Fountain pens." Silence befell the room. "OK, I see a lot of blank stares. I'll try to explain. Many fountain pen barrels, the bodies of the pens, are made of resin. No two look alike. Some are rather plain; many are relatively inexpensive. But a certain percentage of these resins are distinctively beautiful. They are works of art in themselves with properties that make them look like alabaster or highly polished lacquer. Some are uniquely textured. Coloring and striations are such that even the same pen models can be made so that no two look exactly alike. And, of course, the design of the shape comes into play along with the quality and performance of the nibs, the writing tips that bring ink to paper. Ladies and gentlemen, fountain pens are art that writes, just as our products are art that prepares food. Prices range from less than $100 up to the tens of thousands. In many respects, the fountain pen business is a lot like ours. And with the introduction of these new resins that Desi described, it will become more so. And I am supremely confident in our ability to compete and win.

"Desi." He turned to face him. "I know you know that. I also know that you're paranoid about others having the same or better capabilities, that somehow our secrets will leak or that someone else knows things that we don't and is just waiting for the opportunity to exploit their knowledge and bury us. I know you go through personal hell because of your fears. I know these things and I encourage you talk to me about them, because I believe that your paranoia is the fuel that drives you and keeps us at the leading edge. As long as you remain neurotic and don't become psychotic, I'm fine."

"How comforting," said Desi. And as he began to laugh, so did everyone else. When the laughter subsided, Desi went on. "Joe actually makes a great point about our ability to compete and win. I have already begun to experiment with some resins to design a whole new line of products. Serving bowls and trays, even cups and plates. We can create an entirely new line of related products in that category while staying true to our artistic design roots. Of course, that arena is already filled with some strong competitors, and we would be the new kids on the block. But the new resins would enable us to bring an entirely fresh approach to the table, no pun intended. Anyway, I think you can see where I'm going with this, so that's enough for now."

The energy in the room suddenly crackled with excited interest as Joe resumed. "There are, however, some implications in what Desi described that concern me a lot. When we acquired the mid-price lines, we didn't just buy three companies; we bought three different cultures and three different sets of core values. I am coming to realize that those differences are a big part of why we are not yet achieving the success that most of us predicted. We have not done a good job of truly understanding the cultures and the values of the companies we now own. We haven't even attempted to learn what they can teach us about the world they live in and the markets they serve. Instead, we naively marched forward on the assumption that all we had to do was introduce our modified Kitchen Sculpture designs into their markets, and we'd experience an avalanche of consumer acceptance. Off-the-chart sales would just fall from the heavens. We got just enough sales to delude ourselves into thinking that we were on the right track and all we had to do was work harder and whip the people involved harder, advertise more, and success would be a no-brainer. Think about it. We've treated those companies and the people in them like bastard stepchildren from the get-go—and then we wonder why they don't enthusiastically bow to our demands.

"I don't think we're stupid, but I do believe that we've been embarrassingly naive. Why? First of all, other than perhaps Samantha, none of us have any experience in merging different cultures into one. Secondly, we're not doing a good enough job of understanding our own culture and living the core values that we claim to be ours. If we haven't yet gotten our own act together, how can we possibly do a decent job of integrating other cultures? What we've focused on instead are the numbers: sales, earnings, cash flow, and return on investment. We have made keeping score more important than playing the game. And I'm the guiltiest one in the room."

"Joe?"

"Yes, Ben."

"Surely you're not saying that the numbers aren't important. Are you?"

"Of course not. The numbers are always important. But they're the measures of how we're doing at achieving our goals; they're not the goals themselves. Look, we gained dominance in our markets because we developed a deep, intelligent understanding of every facet of that market: our dealers; their customers, the ultimate consumers; the nuances of customer service; aesthetic tastes; the materials that we use to make our products; engineering and manufacturing considerations; et cetera, et cetera, et cetera. If we expect to do the same in the mid-price world, we need to develop and apply the same depth of knowledge that got us where we are in our core business.

"When I realized this, a light bulb went off in my head. I have a much clearer understanding of what our new definition of our Brand really means and how it can help us get there and stay there. The 'what' and the 'how' is really a central gathering place where everyone in our company, no matter where they work or what they do, can understand and commit to a common goal—building and sustaining our Brand. They can see why and how what they do is important and why they are important."

"Joe," Samantha cut in, "in your last statement you just defined the meaning of the word *fulfillment*. And fulfillment is the most essential element there is in having motivated, productive employees. I probably sound preachy and academic, even pedantic, but it's true. Every study ever done bears it out."

Joe glanced at his watch. It was 12:15, fifteen minutes past their scheduled lunch break. "Well," he said, "I really got on a roll there. But a lot of things came together for me in this last hour, and I needed to share them with all of you. Brandon, would you like to say anything?"

"Yes, I would. I'd like to say that this is a good time to break for lunch. Let's cut it a bit short so we can be back here, ready to go at five minutes after one. Thank you all for a most productive morning."

As everyone filed out for lunch, Brandon spent a few minutes reflecting. While Joe was speaking, Brandon was carefully observing everyone's facial expressions and body language. *Interesting,* he thought. *Joe's extemporaneous presentation was emotional, powerful, and right on the money. But some people were not yet on the train. I wonder why?*

The answers needed to come soon. But would they?

Chapter 20
What Not To Do –
Sometimes The Truth Hurts

Lunch had been a tame, quiet event. Everyone was apparently still processing what he or she'd heard over the last portion of the morning session. Conversations were short and superficial. People needed to decompress, and no one was ready to touch anything that was said during the last hour. Not even Joe. So, when they resumed their meeting, Brandon decided to continue to get input and see what came up.

"Erika, you started to speak a couple of times, and I cut you off. Why don't you tell us your thoughts on the new definition of your Brand," said Brandon.

Erika had listened closely to everything that was said during the morning session. She felt that Joe's comments reflected the kind of wisdom she would want to follow. But she was unsure about how certain other people felt, how they would react, and how their behavior would change. More accurately, it wasn't other people; it was one person—Mark Selisman. She didn't trust Mark to tell the truth, to relinquish any power, to become a better listener, or to give a damn about anyone else's ideas or point of view. For her, the bottom line was that Mark was Mr. Passive/ Aggressive; he would say anything he needed to say in order to keep doing what he was doing and not change one iota.

"I think you all know," she began, "that I see the foundation of our Brand as connection; connection between us and our dealers and between us and the end users of our products. And I hope you know that one-way 'push' communications from us to our audience are not the way of the future. People don't want messages; they want conversations. They don't want to be told; they want to be consulted. They don't want cleverly designed images; they want authenticity. Anybody here use Yelp? Do you even know what it is or how it works? I don't want to go into it now. But check it out. You really need to check it out.

"I don't like to talk a lot, so let me bottom-line it. We don't do any of what I just said. We are so lame about communications, it's embarrassing to me. I stopped talking to my friends about our company because I don't want them to go to our website. We're still living in a web 1.0 world. I can't believe it. We could be using social media to do so much to connect with end users, find out what they think about our products, about us as a company, about what they want to see from us. We could use that information directly, and we could use it to help our dealers become more successful. Instead, we do nothing. And here's the reason. Mark Selisman."

Erika stopped talking and stared at Mark with a look usually reserved for serial killers. Everyone froze. Like everyone else, Mark sat, paralyzed. Then a crimson glow began in his neck, rose slowly to the top of his forehead, and slid back to where it began, replaced by an ashen pallor.

"How dare you accuse me of that," was all Mark could manage to spit back.

Joe started to jump in, but Brandon held him back. "This needs to come out in full bloom so we can deal with it, once and for all," he whispered to Joe.

Everyone else remained silent. Instinctively, they knew that this would be a battle between two gladiators; no other voices welcome.

Erika and Mark sat on opposites sides of the table, glaring at each other through eyes boiling with an anger of volcanic proportions.

"You know," Erika released a big breath, "until just now I thought I had written you and the company off, that I had become indifferent and didn't care anymore. I was wrong. I care a lot. I buried my feelings, something I'm good at, and I just scared myself when I felt the intensity of my anger. I'm not sorry for what I said, because I believe it's all true, every word. You are impossible to talk to when it comes to bringing up new ideas or things that you don't agree with. You just won't listen, and you dismiss me or anyone else who has a different take than yours. And I think you are technology phobic, you won't admit it, and the company is paying the price for it. You've got a ton of reasons to not get involved in social media, and they all add up to one big smelly pile of bullshit."

"So much for civil discourse," Joe whispered to Brandon.

"It's OK. It's necessary," Brandon whispered back.

Mark took a deep breath and tried to compose himself. He almost succeeded. "Erika, how long does it take to create a robust social media presence?"

"Depends on your definition of robust."

"Don't play games. How long? A year? Two years?"

"Somewhere in that range."

"Do you understand the time pressure we're under to produce sales results, especially in our mid-price line? Do you have a clue about what it takes to get shelf space and SKUs placed in the stores we sell to? You think that we just compete against other products like ours? Let me give you a little lesson in sales and marketing. When we try to build a relationship with dealers and have them sell our line, those dealers aren't just looking at our products compared to other products that do the same thing. They're looking at how much revenue and profit they can generate in the space they give us versus what they can generate with any other products that might work in their stores. So we're competing against bowls, and vases, and pots and pans, and woks, and exotic spice racks and decorative pillows, and you name it. And those dealers want to know how much we're willing to spend on special promotions, how much we're willing to commit to train their salespeople to sell our products, how generous are our return policies for slow-moving products, what kind of holiday gifts with purchase we're willing to provide, and whatever the hell else they can think up.

"Recently, there's been another factor thrown into the mix: buying groups." Mark was really wound up now. "Basically, they operate like dealer co-ops and do group buying for any given number of retail dealers who join the group. They have become another level in the distribution chain that further erodes our profit. Ben can tell you about the conversations he and I have had regarding how to deal with them. All of that costs us money and reduces our profits. Do you think that the only thing dealers care about is how unique we are? Do you think that I just put a bunch of baboons out in the field, and they walk into a store, and the dealers fall all over themselves to buy our products because Desi designed them? And all I have to do all day is disagree with you and play golf with customers? Is that what you think?"

"I don't know about Erika," said Manny, "but that's pretty much what I was thinking." Sensing that the situation in the room was about to leap over the edge, he jumped in to defuse the anger as only he could. The smiles and muted laughter from almost everyone told him he was right. Even Mark tried in vain to hide a smile.

"Look," Manny continued, "you two are both intelligent, driven people with strong views. You're bound to lock horns at times. Hell, I know I get into it with both of you. Of course I'm always right, but that's another story." More laughter from the group. The tension eased, just a bit. "It just seems to me," he went on, "we'll get a lot more out of this if you could agree on what the issues are and stop tryin' to kill each other."

"The rest of you may be laughing. I'm not laughing yet," said Erika. "But Mark, you do have a couple of good points. You're right, I don't know much about what you actually have to do to sell our products. And I never considered that we're competing for floor space with a bunch of products that are totally different from ours. But dude, that's even more reason for you to listen to me about how we should use social media. I know that it takes time to build a meaningful presence in the social media space. But while we're building our capabilities, we would be doing a lot of listening and learning about what our end users want from us, what they want from our dealers, how they want us to conduct ourselves with them, what they want to see in future products, and stuff like that. Some of that information might be valuable to our dealers. Mark, doesn't that work for you as something you could be giving our dealers that other companies don't have? If that's true, doesn't that help you get a little more of an edge over our competition? And, dude, it doesn't cost that much to do, so it wouldn't be eating up your marketing budget."

"How much is not much?" asked Ben. "And how can we measure the value of that information to our dealers?"

Erika fidgeted a bit before diving in. "I'm going on my gut here, because Mark and I have never sat down and really put together a plan. As you can tell, our conversations went to hell before we ever got close to any serious analysis. But I'm thinking that we could develop a social media presence with just a couple of people who can listen and respond and write some decent blog posts. Yeah, I think two people to start. And not expensive people—like $30- to $40K-a-year people. And we'd have to redesign our website. What we've got now is nothing more than an online brochure. If we build the site on top of the Word Press platform, we could probably do it for less than $50,000. And we'd have an absolute kick-ass website. With that level of investment, we could make serious progress."

Now Mark jumped in. "What exactly does that buy us in terms of delivering unique value to our dealers?"

Erika responded. "How many of our dealers have Web 2.0 websites? How many of them blog? How many are on Facebook and have company pages and connect with their customers?"

"A few of the regional chains, and maybe a handful of the most successful high-end kitchen boutiques."

"And how do those dealers use their social media presence?" asked Erika.

"They promote their stores and the lifestyle they represent. They have classes and demos. They bring in celebrity chefs. Desi has made a few appearances and talked about design. Stuff like that."

"Those are decent ideas, provided they get the turnout they're looking for and the right kinds of input from the attendees about what they want to experience more of. But I'm thinking it sounds like they talk a lot, but they don't spend much time listening and learning from their customers. Is that true?"

"Probably. Yeah, I think so," said Mark.

"OK, here's two things all you guys need to get your heads around. And I mean everyone in the room.

"Ideas. Ideas conceived through customer input and not necessarily thought up by our salespeople or our designers.

"Discussions. Discussions started and perpetuated by customers; not push messages that we, or our dealers, put out, expecting responses from our audiences.

"Our social media presence can generate a body of knowledge about end-user needs and wants, from lifestyle preferences to products and services that support those lifestyles; knowledge that our dealers can incorporate to address their customers' needs. Right now, I'm thinking that there's too much guessing happening. Everyone is making a lot of top-down decisions about what to make and what to sell.

"Ben." She turned to him. "I'm not sure how to measure that the way you would like to see it. But it must be doable because if it works, it will definitely lead to greater dealer sales, and it will give Desi more valuable input about what new products and features we should design, and that's gotta help our sales.

"Mark"—her tone was less angry—"does gathering and selectively sharing that kind of information define value in a way that you can use it?

"Dudes," she said to the entire group, "I know I'm just the nerdy chick who crunches data. I'm just sayin'."

Erika had never before voiced her opinion on a topic of that nature in a group meeting. Everyone needed several minutes to absorb the content and the impact of her words. Joe, in particular, seemed impressed. Brandon smiled as he whispered, "We're seeing another example of moving away from personal attacks and looking at the issues. A real team is emerging. I love it."

Mark calmly rose as he began to speak, perhaps to reassert himself as the self-proclaimed alpha male, or just to clear his head. "Erika, you brought up some potentially valuable points. And yes, I agree with you that our discussions have never gotten as far as they did today. You seem to know quite a bit about social media, and I can see where it can be significant for us. But I need to educate you a bit more, and maybe some of the rest of the group too, on the nature of many, if not most, of our dealers. They don't care much about social media. They are classic, traditional retailers, still selling the way they did in the 1980s and '90s. They want us to give them co-op advertising dollars so they can promote sales and special events and classes and other traditional devices that they've been using forever. I think that what you're talking about can be extremely valuable, but we're going to have to sell that value to our dealers, at least initially. That means training our salespeople."

"That's easily doable," said Samantha. *Whew,* she thought. *At last an opportunity to say something.*

"But it does represent time and money, and we need to know how much of each," said Ben.

"And," said Mark, "I'm not sure that many of our end users are all that social-media savvy, or interested."

"You might be right at the very high end of the market," said Erika. "But what about our mid-price products? The demographic group with the highest number of current and new Internet users is women over the age of fifty. Seems like that's a group we want."

Joe now stood up as well. "Look, people, we've discovered something valuable. We need to examine it and move it forward, but not right now. Erika and Mark, I applaud the breakthrough you've both made here today, not just about the information, but, more importantly, the way you started your conversation and the way it ended."

Brandon added the final touch. "Do you all see how these kinds of things directly influence the *what* and the *how* of your Brand? And how failing to capitalize on your collective strengths weakens your Brand?"

The collective response was a sober silence and bowed heads. Brandon hoped they were processing his words, but he couldn't be certain. One thing he was sure of, however, was that all of them were now beginning to get a sense of what was not working. And although they now knew what not to do, they were not yet ready to grasp what they should do instead. More pain was required.

Chapter 21

Awakening Continues

"Mr. Peacemaker," said Brandon, looking at Manny, "I think it's time for you to speak up. What are your thoughts as to how you can become more directly connected to the *what* and *how* of your Brand?"

Manny smiled. "I've had enough peacemaking practice today to get a job at the State Department. Send me to the Middle East. I'm ready, man."

Appreciative laughter rippled among the group.

"I've pulled my team together, and we've come up with some things that we can do to help strengthen our Brand." Manny's tone was now serious. "They cover three main areas. First, we can work more closely with the production people in our mid-price subsidiaries, learn more about their cultures, teach them more about ours, and help them buy into the need to incorporate a value- and quality-driven approach to manufacturing rather than just fixating on low cost to the exclusion of everything else. Second, we need to do our part to coordinate with Mark and the sales team so we can stay ahead of all the sales activities that are creating production crises today. If we knew in advance what was coming, we could do a much better job of balancing inventories, avoiding stock outs and shipment delays, and lowering our overtime costs. And the third thing is on me. I need to become more flexible about lookin' for cost-effective, innovative ways to build the stuff that Desi designs instead of being so quick to say no. I know I'm too old-school in my approach to building complex tooling, and I'm quick to reject new methods just because I'm not familiar with 'em. I need to be willing to learn more and fear less."

"Anyone care to respond?" said Brandon.

"Yes," said Mark. "Manny, I know we would benefit from the kind of communication you're talking about. I'm just thinking that it might not always be possible to do that. Sometimes, I think that you believe we're holding information back from you on purpose or because we just don't think it's necessary to tell you. I want you and everyone else to know that that's not the case. Sometimes, we don't know about these sudden opportunities and needs any sooner than you do. When we find out, the very first person we tell is you.

"And as far as show and exhibit deadlines are concerned, those dates are usually set a year in advance. You and Desi have more control over meeting those requirements than we do."

"Mark," said Manny. "You ever turn down a special request from a dealer because it just costs us too damn much and doin' it means losing our ass?"

Mark thought for a long minute before answering. "I can't think of one. I guess I never have. Why would I?"

"I just told you why. 'Cause we lose our ass."

"Maybe on that individual transaction. But depending on who the dealer is, and how much we sell them annually, and how our competitors would love to use our perceived lack of support to get more of their product into the dealers' showrooms and lessen our presence, I don't think we have the luxury of saying no. So we suck it up and do the best we can."

"So are you saying that we're just stuck where we are and there's nothin' we can do to improve the situation?"

"Pretty much."

"Mark, I thought after what we've been through today that you turned the corner and were starting to see things through new eyes, but it looks like I was wrong. So just like you gave Erika a little lesson in sales and marketing, I'm gonna' give you one in studying inventory movement and production planning. You're looking at sales from the perspective of our customers. If we're ever gonna' get out in front of the problem we have to look at sales from the perspective of our products and see if we can find some movement patterns that behave in predictable ways. After my meeting with Joe and Brandon, that's just what I had my team do— look for repeatable product movement patterns relating to special sales promotions. And, whadda' ya' know, we found some. We also found, predictably, that the most spontaneous promotions are being done by our smaller, least sophisticated dealers.

"Mark, we can forecast orders for each of our products for special promotions by month for the next twelve months. You and I can review the forecasts, by product, for every dealer involved in special promotions. Then you can use those forecasts to, maybe, plan promotions several months in advance instead of reacting on the spur of the moment. I'm kinda' guessing that better-planned promotions are more successful than spontaneous ones. So you and your team become a better resource instead of someone who just supports mediocre performance.

"What all that does for us should be obvious. We can plan our production, optimize our inventory stocking and turnover, eliminate overtime in production, never have out-of-stock situations, and improve customer satisfaction—and our Brand.

"All that's required is for you to stop thinkin' that your perspective is the only one that matters and start acting like a team player instead of the Lone Ranger."

Mark felt the pressure of seven pairs of eyes fixed squarely on him, waiting, hoping to witness an epiphany. Mark was not, however, a storybook character in a storybook plot with a storybook ending. He would not suddenly abandon habits honed over a lifetime because of a few promising encounters that showed him a seemingly better way. He was still locked in a death dance with his demons. It was a struggle between the forces in his mind, fighting to retain absolute control, and the army of his emotions, wanting to feel and express and belong to something greater than himself. It was a private, deeply personal experience. He was not yet ready to share his transitional trauma. He needed time.

"I'm thinking," he said to no one in particular. Pain had crept into his face. Everyone could sense his struggle, even if they couldn't identify with it. "Brandon"—Mark turned to look at him—"why don't you talk to someone else and allow me to let my thoughts percolate for a little while?"

"Fine, Mark," Brandon said. "I suggest, however, that you allow your emotions into that conversation as well. It might be more painful, but I can assure you it will be more rewarding."

"Sure," said Mark. That would not happen easily. Mark's mind had other plans.

Chapter 22

The Death Dance Of Resistance

For most of the afternoon, Samantha was experiencing her own private awakening. She had come to the retreat with a goal and an agenda. She wanted power, and she needed to recruit allies to help her get it. But as events unfolded, she began to see legitimate needs and opportunities associated with the company's Brand that transcended politics as she experienced it from her prior positions. Kitchen Sculpture was different, she thought. The areas where she could apply her expertise and make a difference were genuine; and she was not encountering the resistance she'd anticipated. The opportunities flowed like water from a spigot. All she needed to do was listen. And listening was one of her strengths. The candid confrontations, the uncomfortable truth-telling, the uncovering of core issues—all these things had enabled her to learn more about her colleagues in one day than she'd learned over the past year.

In just the last several minutes, her most exhilarating realization had rolled over her like a gentle wave; she did not need to be political to succeed. She simply had to be persuasive. She felt a sense of freedom that she imagined a wild animal felt when released from captivity and returned to its natural habitat.

She sensed that the silo mentality that defined the organization was based on fear, not on politics. She saw everyone in the group as fundamentally clean and wanting the best for the company. She believed their problems stemmed from being prisoners of their own narrowly defined experience. They felt trapped on a treadmill of events happening too quickly, leaving no time for deep analysis and creative experimentation. All of that kept them locked in their comfort zones, running at full throttle, fearful of trying new things that might upset their precarious sense of balance. They were the victims of financial success and could not see the rapids looming ahead.

"So, Samantha," said Brandon. "I'm sure you've had a chance to reflect on the new definition of your Brand. What have you come up with?"

"Well first of all, thank you for asking. And thank all of you for giving me the opportunity to be part of this process."

Oh God, she thought. *Why did I get so politically correct? That was dumb. I guess old habits die harder than I thought. Need to work on that.*

At the same time, Joe thought: *Nice touch of good manners, Samantha. We all could use a little more of that.*

Private self-flagellation aside, Samantha continued without missing a beat. "I think that I represent and can influence more of the *how* part of our Brand than the *what.* Even though, as Brandon has pointed out, we are all players and not spectators in strengthening our Brand, I think my impact is felt by what I do to improve our personal interactions with our various constituents."

"Hey Samantha," said Manny. "Could you give us an example in plain English?" His smile said he was only half serious.

"Sure, Manny, and everyone else who might be conceptually challenged." Her smile said she wasn't offended. "One obvious area where our people interact directly with our dealers is sales. I know that we can improve our listening skills, the most important aspect of effective communications. And by doing that, we can improve the quality of our dealer relationships, and because we're relationship-driven rather than transaction-driven, that has to improve the quality of our Brand."

"Whoa, whoa, whoa," said Mark. "Are you saying that our salespeople are not effective communicators? Where do you think they're not effective, and how could you possibly know, one way or the other? And be specific. I don't need to hear a bunch of academic, hypothetical generalizations."

"Ooh, sounds like someone hit a nerve," said Manny, still smiling. "I like this."

"I'm not trying to offend you or our sales team," said Samantha. "And I'm not just talking about our traditional products. In fact I'm speaking mainly about our mid-price line people. We all know that they come from cultures that are price- and transaction-driven. We've even talked here about the need to transition them to become relationship-driven. But to be more specific, I've had some conversations with our regional sales managers over the past three months."

Mark was animated and agitated once again. "Why? What were you doing poking around my sales team?"

"Mark, I wasn't poking at all," said Samantha. "They came to me, all four of them, because they were repeatedly running into situations that seemed to have a consistent pattern and were not achieving the results that they or you wanted. They were frustrated and wanted my opinion."

"Why didn't you send them to me?"

"Because they said they'd spoken to you several times and were still not getting good results. They wanted another point of view. Why is that a problem?" Samantha's agitation was controlled but everyone knew she had now taken the gloves off.

"Then why didn't you come to me and tell me about this at the time?"

"Because all four managers wanted me to keep quiet about it until they'd had a chance to try what we discussed and see how it worked. They were worried about you rejecting any ideas that came from outside your immediate circle."

Joe was too angry to remain silent. "Mark, you are diverting a conversation away from the issue at hand—better communication—and turning it into a discussion about your need to control. That is exactly the kind of silo behavior that I will not continue to tolerate. From anyone." He turned from Mark to the group. "Are we all clear on that? Mark, I guess I should thank you for giving us such a blatantly clear example of what I talked about earlier, but I'm not going to. Samantha, please continue."

In the seconds before she resumed, Samantha thought to herself: *Thanks, Joe; you definitely get it. And this is a perfect example of me not needing to be political, just persuasive. I like this.*

"Well, as I was saying," she continued, "it seems our mid-price salespeople have been conditioned to interact with our dealers with one value proposition—price. In addition, our salespeople tend to talk more than they listen. They go into meetings with their customers and immediately start pitching our products based on accomplishing their preconceived goals of selling a certain number of SKUs. They talk about things like the revenue per square foot that a dealer might realize with our products, the healthy gross margins we offer, our generous return policies, et cetera. Now I realize that with customers like big-box retailers and large department store chains, we're just a number on a buyer's roster of vendors. We're not given much time, and there's little if any relationship beyond the current transaction. But that's not the case with smaller retailers. Yet our sales reps start making that same pitch to them before they even know what the dealer is looking for, or what the dealer's goals might be. It's still a transactional dialogue.

"Our regional managers have also told me that it seems like our salespeople want to get in and out of every meeting as quickly as possible. Speed is their mantra. At the end of the day, they—and consequently, we—know very little about our dealers' businesses. And the companies we acquired had apparently achieved a surprising amount of top-line success with that approach. And we certainly don't want to see revenue slide, so they just keep doing what they've always done. That's my understanding of the situation based on my discussions with our sales managers. How does that compare to your assessment, Mark?"

Mark stared blankly at Samantha with unbelieving eyes. How could she have gotten so much information and interpreted it so accurately with so little interaction, not to mention no background in sales?

"Uh, yeah, Samantha. You understand it pretty well. Uh, just curious; how did you manage to get that much with just one meeting? I assume it was one meeting. Am I right?"

"You're correct, Mark. It's what I'm trained to do. It's really about mostly listening; listening to learn, not to agree or disagree and not to force my point of view into the conversation."

"But you don't have a sales background."

"Mark, I understand what it takes to build relationships. I understand the nature of business. And I got involved in sales situations at my last company. I'm here to help, to add value, to strengthen the *how* of our Brand. I'm not trying to do your job or upstage you."

"So where did you leave it with our sales managers? What are they doing as a result of your meeting?"

"I gave them some questions that they could, in turn, give their sales reps; questions designed to begin a real dialogue with our dealers about their goals and needs. It's about more than offering the lowest price.

Once our sales reps collect enough information, you can begin to design some creative programs for those dealers, something I'm told you excel at; programs that differentiate us and make us more valuable as partners in our dealers' success. That's an example of what I think I can do to strengthen the *how* of our Brand. Mark, Joe, you have already defined the *what;* it's relationships."

Erika chimed in. "This whole listening thing is a good parallel to what I've been talking about in the social media space. The virtual world has the same needs and opportunities. We just address them in a different way. But they're both about listening, learning, and building trust."

Mark sat stock-still, head down, his left hand on the table in front of him, his right massaging his jaw. He was lost in his world of internal conflict. The demons in his mind were running out of steam; they struggled to regain power, but their arguments were less and less convincing.

"I can cite more examples if you want me to," said Samantha.

"You've made your point," said Mark. "And it's a good one."

"We know it's a good one," said Joe. "The bigger question is, do you get it? I mean really get it. Get it as in sharing information, as in asking for input and help, as in not thinking you have to have all the answers, as in not thinking that anyone else in this organization is trying to steal your thunder, as in knowing that admitting your ignorance is a sign of strength, not weakness. Where are you, Mark?"

Chapter 23

A Line In The Sand

Brandon took over before Mark could respond. "Mark, throughout the day you have had exchanges with everyone in this room about behavior that directly affects the *what* and *how* of your Brand. You've heard plenty of examples of what happens when you over-control the activities of the salespeople—when you don't allow the Kitchen Sculpture team to fully contribute their talents to strengthening your Brand and improving your results. And at each turn of the road you continue to resist. What's going on?"

"I'm not really sure, myself. To a large extent, I think the attacks are unfair. But that's fine. I'm a big boy. I'm used to this kind of stuff from people who don't fully understand what my team and I are doing, who have no idea what challenges we face in the marketplace every single day. I know our mid-price products are lagging behind forecasts. I'm the first one to admit it. But we're still in the early stages of learning about that segment of the market. I'm confident we'll pick up the pace soon.

"As far as our core products are concerned, we're on target with our projections. So I don't understand the great concern. I think it's a question of some people just wanting to have a voice in areas that are none of their ...uh, not their responsibility."

"This is such bullshit," said Desi, now standing and dramatically waving his arms in a Desi-esque pattern used only in highly charged situations. "I've been trying to restrain myself for a while, but I can't hold it in any longer. Mark, are you actually hearing the crap spewing out of you? First, you sat there and basically agreed with almost everything being said. You acknowledged that Erika's and Manny's and Ben's and Samantha's and even my ideas had merit. And now you sit there and have the audacity to refute your own words and once again put everyone down in the process. Do you have any idea how shut down you are? How ridiculously resistant to any ideas that are not your own? You are just unbelievable. I'm ready to throw myself off a building just listening to you."

Joe leaned toward Brandon, whispering urgently, "I'm with Desi on this. Where is this going? Do something, or I will."

"I know it sounds bad. Mark is waging an internal war. It's Mark's mind versus Mark's gut. I think his gut will win. I know it's painful to watch, but it's actually healthier to let him have his battle in public. Just let it play out a bit. It will end sooner that way."

"Mark, I agree with Desi," said Ben. "And let me add something about meeting our projections. For the last two years you have fought to reduce our revenue forecasts. You've made a case that we are maximizing our potential in a market segment that is not especially robust and that we cannot expect to continue to grow at the same rate that we have enjoyed in previous years. I have reluctantly gone along against my instincts. I know we're in a unique segment, and there's not much data available, so I've kept quiet. But when I look at sales of other luxury products where price is no object, I see robust sales growth, way better than ours. So I might as well say it outright; Mark, I think you've been sandbagging to make it easier for you look good by meeting unambitious projections. And based on what I've heard today, I think there are things that you don't have answers for—and rather than reach out to the rest of us, you get us to lower our expectations. Not only do our results suffer, but our Brand does as well. I'm telling you right now, I will not roll over so easily in the future."

It was Erika's turn now. "So, Mark, are you telling me that everything I talked about and you said you agreed with before is just a load of crap? Have you completely backtracked? Are you saying you have no intention of following up and going further with my recommendations? Are you really that phony?"

Samantha leaned over to Manny and whispered. "I could say something, but I think it would just be piling on at this point. What about you?"

"Yeah, I feel the same as you," he whispered. "Let's just see what happens next."

"Mark," said Brandon, "up to now, you've done a great job of listening to a lot of things that I know were difficult for you to hear. You have publicly acknowledged the legitimacy, the accuracy, and the value of what your colleagues have had to say. You told everyone that you're on board. And then, over the last few minutes, your statements contradicted everything. They, in effect, made a mockery of today, and of your integrity. You had everyone in the room pulling for you, Mark—and in a matter of minutes you became a pariah. Do you understand that perhaps you've come too far to turn back?"

"Mark," Joe piggybacked on Brandon's words, "I have to tell you and everyone else what's on my mind. I have always respected you and supported you. I think you have an amazing talent and boundless energy for what you do. I still want to feel that way. I say want to, because that is my desire, but it is not my current reality. We all saw and heard the same things today. But we have not all internalized them the same way. We're all unique individuals. We have different points of view. We process information through our own experiential filters. Right now, Mark, I can safely say that it appears that your filters are not only different than anyone else's in this room, but out of sync as well.

"You have some serious thinking to do, Mark. Because as much as I respect and value your talents, and as much as I admire you as an individual, I must tell you that no person is bigger than this organization, or our values, or our Brand. It is now crystal clear to me that our marketplace defines us based on *their* perceptions of the *what* and *how* of their experiences with us. We are our Brand, and our Brand is us. That goes for everyone, including me. Do I have to spell it out more clearly?"

The silence hung heavily, a shroud that prevented the weight of Joe's words from escaping. No one looked up or spoke.

Several minutes went by before Brandon stood and addressed the group. "OK, folks, it's close to five o'clock, and I think we've come to a good place at which to end today's session. Here's what I want you all to do between now and eight o'clock tomorrow morning. The first thing we're going to do tomorrow is to redefine your Brand, based on everything we've learned today. We'll put all your thoughts on the table for consideration, examine all of your ideas, refine them, boil them down to their essence, and come together around what you want the world to believe about what you deliver and how you deliver it.

"Once we've done that, we'll spend the rest of the day looking at ways that you can be and remain the very best of that 'what' and 'how.' I expect to have a productive day. I hope you do as well. And I hope today was enlightening and productive for all of you. I know I speak for Joe as well in thanking you for your candor and your commitment. And with that, I wish everyone a good evening."

Chapter 24
Crossroads

Silntly, everyone filed out of the room. The significance of Mark's sudden reversal and Joe's words remained at the forefront of everyone's thinking. The organization as a whole and Mark as an individual had reached a point of no return. Mark's inexplicable and sudden reversal puzzled everyone. What no one realized was that it was also a puzzle to Mark himself.

Brandon and Joe left the room together. "Want to have a glass of wine and debrief?" asked Brandon.

"Mandatory," Joe said.

They didn't speak until they were seated at a secluded table in the bar. "Your words were timely and appropriate," Brandon said.

"Thanks. I meant every word. I hope I won't have to do the unthinkable and ask Mark to leave. You might not realize how much good he has done for our company. His loss would be tragic. Especially now with the transition we're going through."

"There's never a good time to lose a valuable resource. But just in case it comes to that, ask yourself what would happen to the rest of your team's energy, creativity, and productivity if Mark were allowed to stay on his terms and not change?"

"I know. The whole situation is tearing me up. You know, during the day, when Manny was making his points, Erika was making her points, and Samantha was making hers, I was sitting there thinking that a lot of the things they were saying were things that I thought Mark knew. I mean a lot of it is management 101 stuff."

"You're right, Joe. And I think that Mark does, in fact, know those things too. But you've got to realize that everyone in your organization is running at full speed, you're focused more on numbers than relationships, you've got three new cultures to integrate, you're not getting the results you expected, profit margins are shrinking ... do I need to go on? Typically, when you're in that kind of situation, people have no time to think, to analyze, to step back and reflect on what's happening and why. They just try to work faster and harder, hoping that doing more of what doesn't work will somehow bring about better results. I believe that someone smarter than you and me, whose name I can't remember, once defined that as insanity."

"Thanks, Brandon. On top of everything else, I really needed to hear that. Now my day is truly complete." Joe sardonically lifted his wine glass in a toast. Then, seriously, he said, "What's your take on Mark? Do you think he'll make the turn and come back into the fold?"

"It's harder to predict than I thought it'd be," said Brandon. "I thought he'd have been with us by now. Apparently, the roots of his beliefs run deep. But, Joe, you've got to realize that it's out of our hands now. Mark is in a battle within himself. I just hope he realizes that if he leaves, his issues will leave with him and will spring to life wherever he goes."

While Joe and Brandon were busy debriefing, Mark walked despondently to his room, feeling more alone than he had ever felt in his life—more alone than in his darkest days at prep school, a young boy of privilege whose successful parents were able to give him everything but the thing he wanted most—their time. It was at that school that he taught himself the skills to get people's attention and time—control everything. Make people come to you. Manipulate events so they can't function without you. Those skills had served him well, he thought. Up until today. Now his entire life was at a crossroads. He could not remember feeling more powerless than he did in this moment.

Chapter 25

The Courage Of Surrender

Brandon stood before the group at precisely 8:00 on Sunday morning. The energy in the room exuded anxiety, yet everyone seemed well rested—everyone except Mark, whose droopy, bloodshot eyes and semi-combed hair told the story of a sleepless night.

"First of all," Brandon began, "I want to acknowledge all of you for the work you did here yesterday. I don't know if you're aware of it or not, but together you developed an incredible body of data that will enable us to redefine your Brand and develop a solid approach to sustainably strengthen it. So let's begin by reviewing what you came up with."

Before Brandon could get the next word out, Mark stood up. "Brandon, and everyone, before you begin, I've got something I need to say. May I please do that?"

"Of course."

"I'm sure it's pretty obvious that I didn't get much sleep last night. I'd like to tell you what I did with my time. I spent it trying to process and analyze everything that happened yesterday: your comments, my responses; your anger, my anger; your ideas, my rejections and defenses for what I'm doing; why I feel and believe the way I do; what I might want to change, and what I wouldn't be willing to change. I went through it all. Every single detail. Around one in the morning, I made a painful decision. I decided to resign."

A collective gasp hit the room. All eyes were transfixed on Mark. For a long moment there was dead silence. Finally, Manny managed to sputter, "You've gotta' be kidding."

"Dude, you can't be serious," said Erika.

Joe leaned over and whispered to Brandon, "I can't believe I'm hearing this. Now what?"

Before anyone else could speak, Mark began again. "Wait. Let me finish, please. After I made my decision, I lay down and tried to get some sleep. Two hours of tossing and turning later, I gave up. I couldn't get rid of the twisting pain in my gut. My stomach felt like a wet rag being wrung out to dry.

"So I went for a walk. An hour later this realization hit me. Of course, it was there all the time, but I wouldn't listen. At first I thought I was being weak, letting my emotions overpower my logic. But finally I realized I had it backward. It was my mind that was making me weak. My emotions were trying to tell me the truth.

"I've never allowed myself to have that kind of experience before. I've always believed that showing emotions in stressful situations was a sign of weakness. And I refused to be weak, ever.

"The truth that I tried to avoid, the truth that I tried to tell myself I should ignore, that I thought made me weak, was simply that if I left, I would be leaving for all the wrong reasons. I would be leaving to avoid facing my problems, and those problems would follow me wherever I went. The truth is that I've been suppressing my problems out of fear, not strength."

The group sat, mesmerized by Mark's uncharacteristic speech. He went on.

"I also need to tell you that during those first few hours of self-examination, I was angry at all of you for what I saw as you telling me how to do my job, for giving me ideas that I didn't want or need, for trying to deprive me of control over my area. Then, I suddenly remembered something that happened to me more than twenty years ago.

"Soon after I graduated from college, I went to work as a sales rep for a good-sized sales agency with a sterling reputation for professionalism. The co-founder and managing partner of the agency was the most empathetic, charismatic, ethical person I had ever known. Everyone believed that he was the primary reason for the agency's reputation and success. His efforts probably brought in ninety percent of the agency's clients. The rest of us were responsible for taking care of and selling the products of our clients' companies.

"Well, as it turned out, the managing partner—Mike was his name—liked me and took me under his wing. I was in heaven. One thing that Mike liked to talk about was what he described as the extraordinary abilities of his partners—there were five of them—and the superb capabilities of the entire staff. He never talked about himself. One day, when just the two of us were having lunch together, I asked him why he gave the others so much credit when it was obvious to the world that it was Mike who was the superstar and everyone else was just a supporting player. He gave me a stern stare, a look I had never seen from him before. He asked me where in the world I got that impression and, before I could answer, he quickly told me that wherever I got it, it was utter nonsense."

" 'Mark,' he said. 'Without these guys, I'm nothing. The truth is, I'm just a spokesman, a front man. The real substance of this organization comes from the work they do. And don't you ever forget it. It makes me angry that someone would give you that impression, and that you would buy it.'

"We never discussed it again."

"But Mark," said Samantha, finally breaking Mark's revealing narrative, "I would think that Mike's message would have made you believe and behave totally differently from what we're seeing. What did you do with Mike's message? Why didn't his words shape your conduct? You looked up to this man; he was your mentor."

"You're right. But the truth is, I thought he was being modest to protect his partners. I simply didn't believe him. And to this day I don't know why. But after last night, I know this. None of you are trying to undermine me in any way. All of you are just trying to support me, to support us as a team, and to support this company. And in addition to your good intentions, you have different perspectives on our issues and opportunities, you have areas of expertise and knowledge that I don't have, and I've been a fool not to value what you have to say."

This outpouring of truth telling made Mark feel shaky. While he was copping to his feelings, he didn't want them to get the better of him. He paused, took several deep breaths, and fought to regain his composure. "There, I said it. That was way worse than my worst confession—and I'm not going to tell you what that was, so don't even go there. I think you can guess the rest. I'm staying. I'm not resigning. You guys are stuck with me, unless you have other ideas, Joe."

The cheers and the standing ovation knocked down whatever remained in place of Mark's usual defenses. He didn't try to fight the tears that welled up, the first happy tears he had shed in many years.

As everyone finally settled down and sat, Joe remained standing. "Mark, this is great news, and I congratulate you on your willingness to fight through your fears to find a deeper truth and for the courage to tell all of us. It speaks volumes about your character. I've never been prouder of you than I am right now. But there are still some things you need to tell us."

"I know that, boss. I'm really anxious to tell you all about the rest of my night, and I think that will answer the questions that you all probably still have.

"When I realized that I needed to stay, I suddenly felt this inner calm, the kind of peace I was expecting to feel when I had decided to resign three hours earlier. Then I started to think about how and what I need to change and the kind of person I want to become. That consumed the next few hours. I thought about all the things you guys told me yesterday, and what an asshole I was for rejecting everything you said. It didn't matter whether your comments were valuable or not. The point for me was that I wasn't going to lend them any credence no matter what. When I realized that, it scared the hell out of me. It made me think about how many good ideas I've rejected over the years from God only knows how many people—ideas that could have made me better, made the outcomes better. I just wanted to shoot myself. So I beat myself up for an hour or so. Then I got back to business. The past is over. What about the present?

"I can't tell you I'm a changed man and things will be different starting today. But I can tell you that I am committed to changing my behavior. I'm committed to being a real team player, to listening, to being open, to exploring new ideas, especially the ones I don't agree with. And now, for my second courageous statement of the day: I need your help; I can't do it alone.

"Good grief, look at me. I'm dripping with sweat just from asking you for help. If you guys have any thoughts on how this can work, I'm all ears."

"Just remember what you went through and what you've just told us here," said Manny. "You're committed. You're gonna' screw up and fall off the wagon, so to speak. I get that. But when you do, get back on and keep your promise."

"How about a code word that we can use to remind you when you're not behaving?" asked Ben.

"How about, *Hey Asshole?*" said Erika.

"At least I can understand the logic in that," said Mark. "I still can't get my head around 'Dude.' Who in the world invented that?"

"Here's one," said Desi. "*WhatHow*. I mean, our purpose here is to strengthen our Brand, right? So every time Mark gets off track—or anyone else for that matter—with anything that has adverse implications for our Brand, just say, 'WhatHow.' "

"That works for me," said Mark.

"Oh my God, did everyone hear that? Mark just said yes to something I suggested without an argument. Mark, you really are a changed man. This is fantastic." Desi rubbed his hands together in glee. "I haven't felt this kind of satisfaction since the time I told my mother-in-law that she was a snobbish, self-absorbed, narcissistic bitch."

"Oh my God," said Samantha. "Did you really say that?"

"I did indeed."

"How did she respond?"

"She looked me straight in the eye and said, 'What's wrong with that?' "

"You're kidding. I bet the two of you haven't spoken since."

"On the contrary, Samantha. It changed our relationship for the better from that moment on. We have been totally honest with each other ever since. And we discovered that we actually like each other."

"Brandon, this is getting way off the subject," Joe whispered. "We need to get back on track."

"Relax, Joe, you're watching some real bonding taking place. Your team is starting to come together on a more personal level. There's a big difference between being civil and being personal. Personal is better."

"Any other suggestions?" Mark asked. Silence. "Well, then, let's go with Desi's idea of WhatHow."

Nods all around.

"There's one more thing I have to tell all of you. When I initially decided to resign, I honestly thought that all of you would be happy with that decision. And when I changed my mind and decided to stay, I thought you'd be angry. I'm blown away by your support. I've never been accused of being humble, but I've got to tell you that I have never felt so much gratitude, or felt so much a part of something, as I do right this minute. I want you to know that I'm proud to be a part of this company and this team, and I will do everything in my power to earn your respect."

"Mark," said Manny, "I said this yesterday, and I meant it. You're an intelligent, capable guy. You work hard, you're creative; you've done a lot of good things here. We want you to be here. And it's great to know that you have a plan to become even greater."

"Hear, hear," said Ben. "Hear, hear," came the chorus of replies from everyone in the room.

"I just want to add," said Manny, "that in the course of becoming greater than you are, if you don't become a little more modest in the process, I will personally beat the crap out of you. And I won't use code words to do it."

"I hear you loud and clear," said Mark.

Brandon stood. "I want to mention something that I find interesting. It's about labels, the kind we attach to people and their behavior. I know you have values that speak to personal behavior, like honesty, trust, integrity, and teamwork.

"Mark has exhibited certain behaviors that have earned him the labels 'arrogant' and 'stubborn.' Desi has acquired the labels of being dramatic and temperamental. Manny is considered conservative and stuck in his ways.

"Let me point out that all of their respective behaviors are essentially the same. But the labels you've given them have quite different connotations. And I think it's fair to say that Mark's labels are the harshest."

"Brandon," Samantha interjected, "I think the main reason for that is the way in which each of them present those behaviors. Presentation matters far more than words."

"Good point. But let's not forget that all of you are professionals," Brandon replied, "and you are the senior executives of this organization. Just consider that you have the responsibility to see through the facades of presentation and look at the issues as they really are and not what they superficially appear to be.

"You achieved a major breakthrough this morning. I applaud all of you. Now it's time for a break," said Brandon. "Take ten, people. Nice work."

The team bounced out of the room, happier than at any time during the retreat. Joe and Brandon stayed back as everyone exited to the lobby. "Brandon, I'm ecstatic," said Joe.

"It was the breakthrough you needed," said Brandon. "I'm proud of this group. And I'm especially proud of Mark. He showed real courage. I'm looking forward to what we're going to do next."

Chapter 26

Holistic Awareness Begins

As soon as everyone settled down at their spots after the break, Brandon addressed the group. "Before we start examining the revised definition of your Brand, I'd like to comment on some things we experienced yesterday and this morning.

"First of all, you may still be questioning how some of the things we discussed have any connection to your Brand. Based on the conventional, marketing-driven definition of a Brand, they don't. But conventional wisdom emphasizes awareness, promises, and the various advertising and public relations campaigns and messages that drive them home. What we've been addressing during our time together is the HOW and, to some extent, the WHAT of your Brand. HOW do you deliver on the promise of your Brand? HOW do you deliver experiences to your dealers and your end users' that go beyond satisfaction and create lifetime loyalty? HOW do you create and sustain a culture that understands how everyone's behavior affects customers' expectations, satisfaction, and loyalty? The *what* of your Brand connects to product and message; the *how* is about behavior and execution. The *how* is less glamorous, but it runs deeper. And in the long run, it just might be more significant.

"Another important experience of yesterday involves the dynamics of team play. You began the day in what I call 'attack and defend' mode. And you weren't attacking and defending your points of view about the issues raised; you were attacking each other. It was personal, unproductive, and ugly. To your credit, however, by the end of the day you moved away from personal attacks to attacking the issues, not each other. You grew as professionals and you began to bond as a team, a far more productive MO. You set the stage to move from mere civility to genuine, mutually respectful collaboration. You put yourselves in a better position to truly live your values.

"Of course, we all know what happened with Mark yesterday, last night, and this morning. Mark went to hell and back. He searched for and found his integrity amid the muck of his misconceptions—and he became stronger for it. The rest of you told your personal truths, vented your anger, and when it was done, you were able to recognize Mark's strengths. This morning you stood solidly with him. Not only that, but you worked out a way to continuously support Mark's growth and improve your collective strength in the process. That was inspiring.

"Which brings me to perhaps the strategically most significant thing you accomplished thus far. Because our discussions encompassed both the WHAT and the HOW of your Brand, the very essence of what you brought to the table recognized the quantum nature of your Brand. What I mean by that is that everything affects everything else. Nothing that anyone in your organization does is neutral, or invisible, or unimportant with respect to its ability to influence the image and expectations of your Brand. Excellence in your shipping department can have as much impact as an effective advertising slogan. Credit decisions that support customer relationships can do as much to bolster your Brand as sponsoring a dealer's promotional event. Having the non-salespeople throughout your organization trained to be empathetic listeners and effective speakers will influence people's opinions of your Brand in the same way that your most charismatic salespeople do. Once again, everything affects everything. Everything is either positive or negative. There are no neutrals.

"These are the things that you brought up that have moved you from a traditional discussion of Brand to this more all-encompassing, more quantum place.

"To begin with, there are still problems that exist from your old paradigm. One thing that jumped out at me was the discussion of your core business versus your new mid-price product subsidiaries. The cultural and Brand disconnect you expressed puzzles me. I could better understand it if those subsidiaries made unrelated products for an entirely different industry. But they don't. Functionally, they make the same stuff as your traditional business makes. I'm not certain, but it's possible that with respect to your large retail dealers, you might even be selling to different buyers in the same companies.

"The good thing about this for me is that we're having this conversation within the context of your Brand and not in a somewhat more detached discussion of marketing strategy. This issue demands the broadest approach possible; your challenges touch many areas: marketing, product design, manufacturing, finance, training, cultural integration—all of it. I understand your initial rationale for making these acquisitions: the best candidate for knocking off your products is you. The problems quickly surfaced, however, when you didn't go further in your strategic thinking. It's probably obvious to you all at this point that you did not ask and answer some important questions about your Brand when it came to your new acquisitions. I really appreciate how you brought those issues to light. By doing so, you can see the entire picture clearly, and you can address your needs and opportunities in the most comprehensive way possible. That will enable you to save time, money, and heartburn.

"Correct me if I'm wrong, but in listening to the various conversations that took place yesterday and today and in our earlier private meetings, I got the impression that the pace of your negotiations and the speed with which you saw the need to make these acquisitions was driven by financial considerations and by perceived competitive pressures. In other words, if you waited, you would end up paying a higher price, and more competitors would have gotten a foothold in that segment of the market. Is that correct?"

"Essentially yes to both of those points," said Joe. Ben and Mark nodded in agreement.

Brandon continued. "Well, then, I think it's safe to say that you didn't do much due diligence in the areas of examining the cultures of the companies you acquired: looking at their selling process; their unique selling propositions; the quality of their dealer relationships, and whether or not they were relationship-driven or transaction-driven; their attention to quality control in manufacturing; and a host of other qualitative elements. Instead, you looked at the numbers, made internal assumptions about how you could improve them, ran some financial projections, did some return-on-investment calculations, came up with prices and terms, and negotiated what you thought were some real bargains. Is that pretty much it?"

"Sounds as if you were in the room with us," said Joe.

"Well," said Brandon, "now that you own some problems that came wrapped as opportunities, you really have no choice but to spend the time needed to fix them.

"I know that your immediate instinct is to beat yourself up over what, in hindsight, were mistakes that a first-year MBA student would not make. Don't do that. It would be useful, however, to recreate the conditions that existed when you made your decisions, and consider why those conditions seduced you into acting in ways that now seem to have been embarrassingly inept. In other words, let *me* beat you up.

"I think the culprit was a false sense of urgency. You created an imagined need for speed—speed to prevent another buyer from coming into the picture; speed to prevent another manufacturer from gaining a competitive advantage. So you put yourself under a fictional time constraint that prevented you from doing your homework. You told yourself that whatever problems might arise were minor and easy to solve.

"Ben." Brandon turned to the CFO. "I'm sure, had you taken a few minutes to think about it, you could have negotiated an agreement whereby the companies you acquired would have given you exclusive purchase rights for the period of time necessary to complete your due diligence."

"I'm already embarrassed enough," said Ben. "Do you have to rub it in?"

"Why didn't you buy the time?"

"I didn't want to pay the fees typically associated with those kinds of agreements. I was being cheap."

"OK," said Brandon. "We can go on ad nauseam with this. As I said, we're just trying to recreate the conditions that existed when you bought these companies. You *invented* a set of circumstances that mandated that you act quickly, but those circumstances either did not exist or, if they did, you could have mitigated them. By the way, that's a fairly common set of circumstances for many companies aggressively pursing perceived opportunities.

"Here's what I want to get to. Suppose you had looked at these acquisitions in the context of thoroughly examining them through the lens of our new definition of your Brand. What did the Brands you acquired mean in their markets? What were the beliefs about what they delivered and how they delivered it? How did those Brands compare with your Brand? What were the similarities and the differences? What value could you add to their Brands besides your ability to improve their product designs? What would be your investment cost to do that? How much would that increase their sales? What would your sales and earnings projections look like under those scenarios?

"Those are just some of the financial and sales questions. There are a whole slew of 'how you deliver' questions. Those companies do not have the luxury of selling products in a market where customers have no price constraints. When the only real buying criterion is desire, you play in rarified air. Desi, you must realize that you have been living in design paradise for quite some time."

"I'm aware," said Desi. "Keenly aware. That's one reason why I stay connected to the academic world, so that I can stay ahead of the curve on what the future of design and materials will look like and what they will cost."

"So with respect to the 'what' of your Brand, Desi, these acquisitions suddenly thrust you into a world where price matters. You found yourself culturally unprepared. But instead of stepping back and looking at this within the context of your Brand, you charged ahead, came down hard on the sales force of your newly acquired companies, force-fed them the idea of appealing to the aesthetic sense of the middle class without even knowing what that is, and told yourself that the solutions to your problems are bigger whips and greater effort.

"I know this must sound like I'm still flogging you, but I need to make my point with the greatest amount of force possible, because it's that important.

"Ladies and gentlemen"—Brandon turned from Desi to the group— "one of the most profoundly impactful aspects of this new definition of your Brand, one of its most valuable elements is—CLARITY. I'm talking about a kind of clarity that can give you an accurate picture of the difference between what you want to be and what you actually are in the minds of the people in your marketplace.

"To get a better sense of what I'm saying, let's look at your new companies and examine their Brands."

Brandon walked to the whiteboard and drew a vertical line down the middle. On the left he wrote the heading: IDEALS. "What do you believe they should deliver?" As people spoke, he wrote down their comments.

Desi: "Elegant design at an affordable price."

Manny: "High-end performance at the lowest possible price."

Mark: "The best design; the most advanced features; the fastest-selling, most profitable, easiest to use, best-supported products in their category. I'm looking at this from the perspective of our dealers, not just the end users."

"OK," said Brandon. On the right half of the board he wrote the title: CURRENT REALITY. "Now, tell me what you believe you are actually delivering right this moment?"

"Decent quality, decent prices, so-so product support, me-too design—with the exception of a few more elegant models that we designed after the acquisitions," said Mark.

"Is that just your perception, Mark, or is that a widely held opinion in the marketplace?" asked Brandon.

"I think it's widely held."

"Anyone see it differently?" said Brandon, as he looked around the room. No one spoke.

"Then that's your Brand. It's as simple as that," said Brandon. "It's never what you say it is. It's always what the market says it is. And markets vote with wallets, not words."

"Brandon, based on what you've said, I think we have another reality to address," said Mark.

"What would that be?"

"I think we have to understand how many Brands we actually have, because it's becoming clear to me that we have more than one. At least, that's how I'm starting to see it. Anybody else care to comment?"

Mark's observation created an unexpected, contemplative silence. As people gathered their thoughts and began forming their responses, Joe sensed that his time was now. He slowly rose from his chair, walked purposefully to the head of the table, and methodically looked everyone in the eye, one by one.

"Folks," he said, pain etched across his forehead, "I have remained silent for too long. It's time for me to say what has been bubbling up inside of me for months."

Chapter 27

Confession

"For the past two days," Joe began, I've watched and listened as you all progressed from attacking each other to identifying and addressing the real issues we're facing. You made me proud.

"I've listened to you grumble about how we have remained stuck in silo mentalities even though we all know it's toxic, it's unproductive, and none of us wants to be there. And you each took your share of the responsibility for creating that reality. I saw the drama between all of you and Mark. I sat on pins and needles as Mark went to the edge of self-destruction, had the insight to find the goodness within himself, the courage to break with his past, and the willingness to share his journey with all of us. I watched us all embrace him, warts and all, welcome him back to our team, and promise to continue to support him. It was a pivotal moment for all of us and for our company. It showed me, and I hope all of you, the best of who we are.

"All of that has also shone a light on something that has yet to be done. The fundamental problem has not been laid where it belongs: with my lapse in leadership. I don't know if that's the result on your parts of fear, misplaced respect, or just plain not seeing the issue for what it is."

"Wait a minute, boss," said Manny. "What are you talkin' about with this lack of leadership stuff? You're a great leader. Hell, I'd follow you up any hill. And I think I speak for everyone in this room." All heads nodded in agreement. "Look, we've had some major challenges in the last couple of years. I know you've tried your damnedest to get a handle on things, and—"

"Stop right there," said Joe. "You just said the magic word. *Tried.* Manny, do me a favor. Try to pick up that water glass on the table in front of you." Manny gave Joe a puzzled look, reached in front of him, and lifted the glass. "Stop," said Joe. "Put it down. Did everyone see that?"

"See what?" said Desi. "You asked Manny to pick up the glass, and he picked up the glass. What are we supposed to see?"

"Anyone care to jump in?" said Joe. "Do the rest of you agree with Desi?" All heads nodded yes.

"Manny," said Joe. "I asked you to *try* to pick up the glass. I didn't tell you to actually pick it up."

"I don't see the difference, Joe. You told me to try to pick it up. I picked it up. What am I missing here?" Manny scratched his head.

"The difference, Manny, is between *trying* and *achieving.* They are not one and the same. And sometimes, *trying* is a word we use to make us look good while failing to actually accomplish what we need to do; what we're paid to do; what we've committed to do.

"How about the rest of you?" Joe asked. "Do you understand what I just said?"

"I understand what you said, and I understand what you mean," said Mark. "I think you're saying that we've been hiding behind the word *trying*, and we're not accomplishing what we've—"

"Mark, stop," said Joe, raising his hand as he spoke. "I'm not talking about all of you. I'm talking about me. I'm telling you all that I haven't done my job as a leader, that I let all of you down, that I let our company down. It's easy for me to sit back, watch you go through the process we've gone through yesterday and today, and to somehow disengage myself from the responsibility for our failures. But that's perpetuating a lie."

"Hey, boss," said Manny. "Don't ya think you're being a little too hard on yourself? I mean, we're all in this thing together."

"Manny," said Joe, "I'm not normally into self-flagellation, so don't try to deprive me of the same pleasures most of you have experienced here."

"Now you're talking," said Desi. "Go for it, Joe."

When the laughter died, Joe continued. "OK, folks, let's break our situation down. We've been complaining about the fact that we've been operating with a silo mentality. We know it's wrong, and yet we've remained stuck there. I've known about it for as long or longer as any of you. What have I actually *done* to improve us, to change that reality and move us to a more collaborative way of running our company and doing our jobs? I'll tell you what. *Nothing.* I've verbally acknowledged it, commiserated from time to time with all of you, told you that I didn't like it and that we should stop being that way. But actually doing something? Hah. I've been MIA. And oh, by the way, whose responsibility is it to lead us in a different direction? Mine.

"Now let me say a few words about our favorite dartboard, Mark. Mark is charged with the responsibility for sales and marketing. If things are going well in that area, Mark typically gets too much credit, and if they're going badly, he gets too much blame. It's kind of like being a quarterback in the National Football League. But how many of you truly understand what Mark does, what challenges he and all of us face in the marketplace? And if you did know—as you should— how might that change your behavior, the kinds of questions you ask, the shape and extent of the support you provide, the teamwork you develop?

"Whose responsibility is it to properly explain what Mark's, and for that matter, every one of our roles is, in driving our business and building our organization? It's *mine*. And who abdicated that responsibility and left it up to all of you to figure out among yourselves? *Me*.

"It's true that Mark was no angel, and that he needed to examine his dark side, come to terms with his issues, and redefine himself. But who created the environment that exacerbated his problems and helped drive our collective descent into dysfunction? *Moi*." As he spoke, Joe caught Manny's furrowed expression out of the corner of his eye. "Manny, don't look so confused. It's just the French word for *me*.

"Merci," said Manny. "I wouldn't have slept tonight if you hadn't explained that. But, Joe, I think you know how to read my wrinkles after all these years. You know I'm processing. And I'm guessing that the rest of you guys are, too."

Heads nodded throughout the room. Joe and Manny had eased the collective tension just enough.

"Now I want to talk about the most important part of my failure," Joe continued, "the part that brought us to this retreat—strengthening our Brand.

"We all know the story of our acquisitions of the mid-price companies. I forced an excessive sense of urgency in closing these deals based on my perceived need for speed to market. Ben, based on my directive, you picked up the pace and took some shortcuts on the financial side that you would not have taken, had I given you more time. That, in turn, forced some other shortcuts in our due diligence and in our analysis of exactly what the hell we were buying and what we would experience in the marketplace. We did virtually no analysis regarding the cultural integration of the companies we acquired or the implications for our new and existing customers vis-à-vis our Brand. I invented a purely fictional sense of urgency. What the hell was I thinking?"

"Don't put it all on yourself," said Mark. "I gave you lots of support. Your message of urgency was pure gold to me. I love operating at that pace. Now that I think about it, it's probably why I unconsciously create the time crunches that drive Manny crazy. But I'm getting off point."

"Not to me, you're not," said Manny, pointing his finger at Mark. "Not to me, buddy. You just framed the agenda for one of our upcoming meetings."

"I know," said Mark. "I could feel your blood rush to your head as the words came out of my mouth. Just remember, Manny, we love each other. Right?"

"I'm thinkin' about it. The jury's still out." But the smile in Manny's voice said loud and clear that he was fine.

"Just for the record," said Brandon, "I love how these conversations are going."

"Brandon," said Manny. "You've been quiet for so long, I forgot you were still here. Nice to hear your voice. How've you been?"

"OK, OK, OK," said Joe. "Let's get back on track, people. The point of all of this is that we need to realize that the root cause of our current predicament is my leadership. I realize that all of us have played roles from a performance standpoint, but I created the foundation, I set the agenda, and I failed to do what a good leader should have done to rein in my mistakes before they reached these proportions. It's just that simple. And I need to publicly acknowledge what I've done, apologize to all of you, and commit to doing a far better job going forward."

"As far as our Brand issues with our recently acquired companies are concerned," Joe continued, "Mark asked a great question: How many Brands do we have?"

As if on cue, Brandon stood and began to speak. "Before we attempt to answer that question, we need to establish our approach, because we have come to the core of what we are here to do. And our approach is critical. The key to success lies in asking the right questions. If we ask the wrong questions, even the best answers will lead us to failure.

"So the next thing we're going to do is to determine the right questions to ask ourselves. The answers to those questions will enable us to address Mark's point as to how many Brands we have or want to have."

Chapter 28

Preparation For Re-birth

"OK, let's start throwing out some questions to ask ourselves in addressing the issue of what we aim to deliver and how we intend to deliver it," said Brandon as he stood beside the large whiteboard behind the head of the table.

No one spoke. Eyes darted around the room as everyone looked to someone else to begin the process. Rising discomfort eventually generated scattered nervous laughter.

"Don't tell me that after all we've been through for the last two days, every one of you is still too embarrassed to go first," said Brandon. "I can't believe this."

Desi slowly rose, looking uncharacteristically tentative as he began to speak. "All right, I'll start the process. I'd like to talk about how we go about our design process, because I think it closely ties to the kind of questions we want to ask ourselves relative to our Brand." Desi's words came haltingly.

"Yeah," said Manny. "I've always wondered how you guys come up with some of the impossible-to-make designs you give me. Are you gonna tell us what drugs are involved too?"

"OK," said Desi. "I see that I'm going to have to choose my words carefully and use only one-syllable words. But it's fine, Manny. I'm used to doing that with you." Their exchange worked perfectly. The nervousness in the room began to melt.

"I appreciate your willingness to go first," said Brandon. "But why are you so tentative? It doesn't seem like you, Desi."

"We're putting it all together now," said Desi, "everything we've talked about over the last week or so and, of course, these last two days. I don't know about the rest of you, but I've never thought about what my team and I do on the design side as being such an integral part of our Brand. It feels a bit strange to me, and I guess it shows. I feel like this is a test, and I want to get it right."

"I'm pretty sure you don't approach design with this kind of anxiety," said Joe. "Actually, I'm certain you don't, because I've sat in on some of your design sessions, and you and your team express a creative fearlessness that is inspiring. Why is this different for you?"

"I'm not sure," said Desi. "For some reason, I just feel nervous. My stomach is queasy. It's like everything I say has to be right on the mark, or else."

"Or else what?" said Mark, his tone and expression suddenly displaying an intense interest.

As Brandon surveyed the room he noted that everyone was now paying rapt attention to everything Desi had to say, their body language echoing Mark's question.

"This is great," said Brandon.

"It doesn't feel great to me," Desi replied. "Why do you think it's so great?"

"Desi," said Brandon. "You're feeling performance anxiety. The same mix of fear, desire, and adrenaline rush that athletes and performers feel just before a game or performance is about to begin."

"I don't get it," said Desi. "Why in the world would I have those feelings in this situation? I'm not about to do anything resembling a live stage performance or an athletic event."

Everyone nodded in agreement with Desi.

"I think Desi's point is well taken," said Joe. "I don't get the connection either."

"Here's the difference between doing what I asked you all to do in this setting and doing what you've always done before in a different, familiar context," said Brandon. "Last week, when I asked each of you to define your Brand, your answers reflected your personal beliefs, but you were kind of on the outside, looking in. You could offer a definition of your Brand, but *you didn't feel ingrained* in your Brand. Today, you are being asked, for the first time, to state what you intend to deliver based on our new definition, a definition that makes you and what you do an integral part of your Brand. This is not casual conversation; this is the real deal. Desi, your mind thinks *this is* a performance.

"Now perhaps I'm over-dramatizing just a bit. But performance anxiety occurs when you question your ability to deliver, to be good, to thrill your audience. Your brain sends your body an important message that manifests physically—nausea, tension, perspiration, light-headedness, and other forms of discomfort. Pay attention to the symptoms, Desi, because your reaction is telling you that you want to excel, and you care about the outcome. That's exactly what an athlete's or an actor's symptoms tell him as he or she is about to go into an arena or onto a stage. And that's what we're doing now. It's showtime. And that's when the real talent shines."

"So how do we get rid of the butterflies? How do we stop being nervous and get down to business?" Ben had suddenly and energetically reengaged. The others nodded in agreement with Ben.

"By making friends with your discomfort," said Brandon, as he looked around the room and smiled. "When you get that queasy feeling, you know you're in the right frame of mind. It's where you want to be."

"My high school football days are coming back to me," said Mark. "Guys puking in the locker room before we took the field. Then going out and absolutely kicking ass."

"I'm having flashbacks to my childhood ballet recitals," said Erika.

"Your what?" said Manny, his face a mask of disbelief. "Did you say ballet? You, nerdy chick, were a ballerina?"

"Hey, hound-face, I actually had a normal, culture-filled childhood. I even learned to use a knife and fork, unlike some people we know," Erika retorted, mock anger in her voice.

"OK, everyone," said Brandon. "I can see you're getting the point. And the point is that the nervousness is an intrinsic part of the process, and you need to embrace it. It's normal to want to avoid discomfort. But discomfort activates your adrenaline, your focus, and your intense concentration. Discomfort is the doorway to the 'zone'—that magic place where your performance is at its peak, where you see and hear and feel everything, and the world around you moves in slow motion."

"I hate this shit," said Ben. "Now I know why I never liked playing organized sports or being in drama club when I was in school. Make nausea my friend? Are you kidding me? It's disgusting. And besides, we're running a business here. It's based on logic, and critical thinking, and solid analysis. With all due respect Brandon, this is way out in left field. It actually feels silly to me."

"Wait a minute, Ben," said Desi. "I'm the guy on the hot seat right now. And I can see Brandon's point. At least I think I can. Just before all the interruptions started, I was beginning to regain my focus. I wanted to keep going."

"Ben," said Joe, as he stood and walked to the head of the table, as if to reassert his rank. "When you first came here, you and I talked a great deal about your career and what you had accomplished in the field of public accounting."

"I remember," said Ben.

"Do you remember telling me about the time you appeared before the Securities and Exchange Commission to testify about certain accounting practices that your clients had used and that were being challenged by the SEC?"

"Yes," said Ben.

"Ben, there was a lot at stake; a lot of pressure on you to make a presentation that could mean millions of dollars to your client, not to mention the reputation of you and your firm. You did your homework, you prepared well, you rehearsed diligently, and you delivered a great presentation that won the day. How did you feel going into that room, filled with government agency people trying to bury you, other members of your firm judging your presentation, and your client's senior executives expecting you to pull a rabbit out of a hat? What was it like for you?"

"It was everything Brandon just talked about times ten," said Ben. "I had forgotten about that, until you brought it up, Joe. The preparation and the rehearsals all went fine, but as I walked into the room I thought I was going to faint. And then, as I began to speak, I became calm. I knew exactly what I wanted to say and how I wanted to say it. When it was over, I felt like a million bucks."

"A perfect example of performance anxiety," said Brandon. "And the reason your nervousness disappeared and you delivered a great performance is that you shifted your focus away from yourself and toward your audience. You thought about sharing what you knew with them and not about receiving their approval."

"OK," said Ben. "But is there a way to do it without the fainting and the nausea? I hated that part."

"You little wuss." Manny was grinning from ear to ear as he said it.

Ben laughed. "OK, so I'm not a masochist. Sue me."

"I'm sorry, Ben," said Brandon. "That's just the way our minds and bodies work. There's no way to get rid of the jitters and the temporary discomfort that comes with them. It's all part of the performance process. The key is to know that discomfort is a necessary prerequisite to success and to make that discomfort your ally. Because without it, you will deliver a lackluster performance, whether it's in the ballpark or the boardroom."

"May I please finish what I started before I forget what I was going to say?" Desi almost shouted, weaving and waving with his patented Desi-esque flourish.

"Of course," said Brandon.

"Well, for starters," said Desi, much calmer now, "I feel more relaxed. Maybe listening to all of you drama kings and queens helped. Thanks. First of all, when I say *we*, I mean our design team. So, as I was saying, we begin our design process by asking ourselves what we want to create in the way of functionality and performance. We look at what we've done up to now, what our competition is doing, and what is possible with new developments in electronics, mechanics, materials, and technology. That can be a lengthy process. But when we finish, we have only come to a place that I believe is the starting point for what makes us different.

"We are now ready to ask ourselves the all-important aesthetic questions: What kind of artistic, intangible, emotional experience do we want to give our customers? And what do we want them to *feel* when they use our product, and even when they just look at our product sitting idly in their kitchen?

"We list all those feelings and functionalities on a big whiteboard. We envision shapes and themes that will convey those feelings and be able to embody the electronics and technologies to deliver the performance we want. Themes can be serious or whimsical, classic or architectural. Then we begin to draw some prototypes; and we refine and refine and refine them until we get a design that we feel good about: that merges the functional and aesthetic, that differentiates us, and, most importantly, that we know will drive Manny bat-shit crazy. Sorry, Manny, at last I had to reveal our secret."

"Not to worry, Des. I'd be disappointed if you didn't take a shot," said Manny. "But you know, when I really think about it, the truth is that the complexity of your designs has made me and our entire team better at our jobs. You make us stretch and learn. I think it's given us a competitive edge in building the kind of quality we need to go along with the artistic appeal that makes us popular with the high-end crowd. It would make my job so much easier if you gave us straightforward designs that didn't require us to create innovative molds and tooling, and we didn't have to teach our people to use new assembly techniques. But that wouldn't make us different, or better, or able to stay ahead of the pack. So I guess that my bitching and moaning has really become a signal that you're on the money, Des."

Desi and Manny had given Brandon exactly what he needed.

Chapter 29

Preparation For

Re-birth – Part Two

Desi's and Manny's exchange gave the group a good bit of intellectual grist on which to chew. As they sat in silent thought, Brandon rose from his chair and surveyed the room. *They're ready,* he thought.

"Thank you, Desi and Manny," Brandon began. "Desi, you've laid out a great process that all of you can use to define the 'what' part of your product."

"I have?" said Desi.

"Yes, you have."

"And Manny, you've described the essence of what it means and how it feels to stretch beyond your comfort zone, to conquer your urge to take the easy road, and to improve and grow as a result."

"Hey, my pleasure," said Manny. "I was just tryin' to say that Desi's not as big a whack job as we all think he is, but if by chance I added some extra benefit for the team, well, that's great."

"Manny, I expected no less from you," Desi snapped. "Genius is always seen as madness by fools."

"OK," said Brandon, "I see we're back in our groove, so let's move on. I'd like all of you to understand exactly how Desi's process exemplifies the initial step you must all take in answering that fundamental question, *What do we want to deliver, and how do we want to deliver it?*"

Brandon walked to the whiteboard. At the top of the board he wrote: THE THREE QUESTIONS. "I'm going to write three questions that you must ask yourselves. Your answers will become your goals in fulfilling the promise of your Brand."

Brandon turned to the board and wrote:

What kind of experience do we want to deliver?

Then he drew a vertical line down to the bottom of the board, making two columns under the question. At the top of the left column he wrote *Dealers*. At the top of the right column he wrote *Consumers*.

"You will need to address both categories for each of the three questions. It should be clear to everyone, at this point, that there are different behavioral and performance considerations for dealers and consumers. Desi's design process directly addresses this question, primarily with respect to end users. He isn't satisfied with just the *functional* part of 'what' we intend to deliver. He goes on to identify and define the *emotional* experience that he wants our end users to have. That emotional piece is the critical inclusion. Anyone want to tell us why that is?"

"I think I understand," said Joe. "The bottom line is this: *We sell products. Our customers buy experiences.* Their experiences go beyond our products—they embody everything that occurs in the course of interacting with us, and they manifest as feelings. Those feelings become the core of our Brand. The consistency and perceived value of their experiences determines their Brand loyalty. Brandon, I think I now truly understand what you mean when you say that every experience is a Brand experience."

Brandon flashed an ear-to-ear smile. "Joe, you nailed it." He then surveyed the room. "How about the rest of you? Do you see what Joe has described?"

Several minutes of thoughtful silence crept by. Finally, Mark spoke. "I think I get it. I mean I got it intellectually a while back, but after listening to Desi I have a better sense of the actual process they go through. I can see how it applies to what we do in marketing and sales. It's weird, but until today I never actually knew what Desi's approach to design looked like. And I've got to tell you; it's way more involved than I thought it was. Then, hearing Manny made me question my own responses to Desi's over-the-top ideas, not just about design, but about the creative direction he envisions for the company. He definitely takes me out of my comfort zone. Now I'm starting to see that as a good thing, an opportunity to stretch, not just a pain-in-the-ass impediment to me doing my job."

Ben quickly chimed in and told the group how this new reality would guide his actions with their dealers in being more than reliable suppliers, but rather in being seen as true partners. That would mean taking the time to better understand the financial realities, the opportunities, and the challenges of their customers' businesses.

As Erika processed everything that was said, she still saw her role as less integral to their Brand—until she focused on the role of social media in connecting to their dealers and end users. That was her wake-up call. Kitchen Sculpture's newly designed website could become the hub for honest conversations with and between customers, both dealers and end users. Topics ranging from program and product experiences, likes and dislikes, wants and needs, price levels, food preparation, recipes, health, and more could be organized and nurtured on their site. Authenticity on an unprecedented scale could become the new norm. In the Internet world, the new reality was that experiential comments (good or bad) from trusted sources—like real customers—have more influence on buying decisions than advertising and promotional messages. Giving customers a forum for expression seemed like a powerful demonstration of Brand authenticity. Erika was as close to euphoric about the prospects as her introverted, skeptical self would allow.

True to form, her statement to the group was, "I can see the possibilities for strengthening our Brand through a strong social media presence." She said it with the enthusiasm of someone responding to being asked the time of day.

"Wow," said Manny. "Erika is out-of-her-mind excited."

There was no mistaking the meaning behind Erika's steely glare at Manny. She flipped him off with her eyes. Then she smiled. And the room erupted with laughter.

Samantha had not spoken for some time. She was immersed in absorbing everything that had been said: from Brandon's summation of where they had begun and how far they progressed, to his scathing critique of the way they had handled their recent acquisitions, to Joe's mea culpa as to his own leadership failures, to Desi's description of his approach to product design, to Manny's reaction, Mark's observations, and, finally, Ben's and Erika's sense of where they would contribute. With each new disclosure Samantha's excitement grew. She felt as if she had been dropped into "employee development nirvana." Her life's work, her dreams of finding personal fulfillment had just fallen into her lap. All she needed was Joe's support and the appropriate financial resources. She could create a kind of "Brand Ambassador University" and she would become its Dean.

Brandon's voice invaded her musing and brought her into the moment. "Samantha, we haven't heard from you in a while. Where are you with all of this?"

"To be honest, I'm spellbound, overwhelmed, ecstatic," she replied.

"Wait a minute," said Ben. "We've spent the last several hours figuring out that we're unclear on what our Brand means to our customers; we screwed up some important elements of our recent acquisitions, and it will probably cost a boatload of money to fix the problems; and Joe confessed to some major lapses in leadership. And you're ecstatic? Which one of our competitors are you secretly working for?"

"Hey, Bean, way to see the glass as half-full," said Mark. "Maybe you should transfer into sales. We could use a shot of your inspirational attitude."

"Just a little accounting humor," said Ben. "Don't get your shorts all knotted up. Talking like a soprano doesn't become you."

Joe was eager to hear more. "Samantha, time for you to share. What's got you so excited?"

"For starters," she said, "so much of what all of you talked about could benefit from staff training—training that our people are not currently getting."

"I don't see it," said Mark. "Some basic instruction for sure. But training?" Manny and Desi nodded.

Samantha was undeterred. "In addition, we can research existing data that identifies key personality characteristics that are compatible with the Brand behaviors we want our people to exhibit in the course of their work. We'll incorporate those traits into the profiles we look for in making hiring decisions. That will enable us to hire more people who possess the aptitudes to be good Brand ambassadors."

She then went on to define the training and support opportunities she had in mind as a result of listening to the last several hours of discussion:

- Customer service training aimed at: making our employees better problem-solvers; being better at turning customer complaints into opportunities; being more empathetic listeners; and informing callers about our website and encouraging them to go online and get involved in our social-media-generated conversations.

- Developing tailored coaching workshops to help people effectively deal with performance anxiety.
- Making our salespeople more effective Brand ambassadors through better listening skills and a broader knowledge of all the things we can do for our dealers beyond what a prototypical vendor might do.
- Teaching all of our employees the true definition of our Brand and what it means, day-in and day-out, to be a Brand ambassador.
- Developing employee recognition programs to publicize outstanding performance as Brand ambassadors.
- Developing a process for sharing Brand ambassador "best practices" throughout the organization.

"I like it," said Joe. The others nodded, except for Ben.

"Samantha, this sounds like you expect a blank check," Ben cautioned. "We'll need to carefully examine the bottom-line effectiveness of your suggestions and—"

"Stop," said Joe. "We're brainstorming here, folks. Ben, this isn't a budget meeting, it's an ideas meeting."

"Sorry," said Ben. "I accidentally went into my default mode. Carry on."

"Accidentally, my ass," said Manny. "Ben, you only *have* one mode. We always have to talk you down from that ledge. We love you, man but I'm just sayin'." Everyone nodded. *Oh well, no one's perfect*, Ben thought. But his gut told him that he definitely had an issue to work on.

Brandon noticed but did not acknowledge Ben's discomfort. It was a side matter. He knew the group was now moving in the right direction. "Would you like to see the other two questions?" he asked.

Chapter 30

Preparation For

Re-birth – Part Three

Brandon walked to the whiteboard. "OK," he said. "We've explored the first question:

    1.   *What kind of experience do we want to deliver?*

Here are the other two. And he wrote:

    2.   *What will it take to deliver that experience?*

    3.   *Is it worth it—what do we gain by doing it?*

"I think these are meaty questions. Their purpose is to make you dig deep; to create a high level of clarity as to who you can be as an organization, as people; and to help you see your relevance in the marketplace. Answering them, of course, begs many other questions.

"Exploring these questions will help you formulate ideas. Those ideas will form the backbone of strategies to further build your Brand strength. Your effectiveness in executing those strategies will create the reality of an improved Brand.

"Of course, you already have a Brand. You're just beginning to understand what it truly is on an organic level. You clearly deliver *something,* and your customers have formed their opinions about *what* that something is and *how* you deliver it. Up till now you've described what you think is your Brand as seen through the message- and image-shaped lens of the marketing world. But your customers are way ahead of you; they already see your Brand organically. So another way of summarizing our work over these past two days is that its goal is to put you and your customers on the same page regarding your Brand."

"I have a question," said Mark, with a quizzical look. "When we ask ourselves, what does it take? I think we pretty much know what it takes. I mean, we understand the experiential part of the equation. Everyone here has thought about what they have to do in their areas of responsibility to create the customer experiences we want. Aren't we beating this thing to death here?"

Joe jumped in before Brandon could respond. "Mark, it's ultimately about execution," he said. "The best ideas, the best strategies, the best plans in the world don't mean squat if we don't execute them well. Everything we've talked about for the last two days is theoretical if we don't dig into the heart of our organization and examine our capacity, our readiness, and our resolve to execute.

"We haven't begun to discuss teamwork and coordination. For example, we have a checklist of training topics from Samantha but no assessment of our current skill levels in those areas. Where's our starting point? And to Ben's earlier point, what financial resources are we able to throw at this? I could go on for the next hour, but I think you all get what I'm driving at. Yes?"

"Yes," came the collective response.

"Mark," Joe's tone was apologetic, "I didn't mean to jump all over you." Joe turned his gaze to everyone in the room. "I guess I'm more highly attuned to execution because of our time together here. It's been a huge eye-opener for me, and I hope for all of you, too. I think the questions that Brandon has posed require that we take a hard look at how we actually function; at what our results say we do, not just our words. And this idea of focusing on two distinct audiences—our dealers and our end users—has me thinking about some things that we can do in concert with our dealers that we have traditionally left up to our dealers to do by themselves."

"I'm not offended in the least by your comments," said Mark. "But all the things we've covered raises another big question in my mind. Currently, our marketing arm has been responsible for our Brand. Now, we're talking about everyone in our organization being an integral part of our Brand, and I get it; I really do. But if everyone is responsible for the quality of our Brand, doesn't that really mean that no one is truly accountable? And if that's the case, I'm thinking that we're going to look like our government—when something goes well, everyone wants to take credit, and when it goes wrong, everyone points to someone else and no one is ever held accountable."

Brandon and Joe exchanged looks as they absorbed Mark's words. As if prearranged, Brandon rose to speak. "We've spent the last two days talking about your Brand in terms that never touched the role of marketing and sales. That's because their role hasn't changed, and neither has their responsibility. The marketing arm of your company is still the gatekeeper for everything having to do with your Brand. Your message, training, social media, new dealer financing programs, and whatever else comes into being—it all has to include strong communication and coordination links to your marketing arm."

Mark's uproarious laughter filled the room.

"What's so funny?" asked Brandon.

"Yeah," echoed Manny.

"Dude, what's with the weird attitude?" Erika chimed in.

"Care to enlighten us?" asked Joe.

"I'm just drowning in the irony of this entire process, and I guess my laughter is coming from that place of 'be careful what you wish for.' I have one more confession to make. When Brandon first arrived and we had all of our individual meetings, my biggest fear was that I would lose control of my area, I would have a diminished role in the company, and I would be marginalized. It was irrational, and I know that. But it was still real to me. So now we've come full circle and not only am I not diminished, but I have an even larger and more responsible role than I ever imagined. Right this second I'm just numb, but I promise you guys, as soon as it sinks in, I'll be insanely happy. For now, the best I can do is to laugh my ass off."

Joe's attitude was cautionary. "You do understand that it's about added responsibility and not glory. Right?"

"Of course," said Mark. "Joe, and everyone, I know you understand how my life has dramatically changed in the last forty-eight hours. It's all good. But it's a lot to absorb. After the introspection, the self-discovery, the pain, and my reawakening, I can tell you all that this has been, without a doubt, the most gratifying experience of my life. And I'll say it again, I will not let you down."

"Well," said Brandon, "on that note, I think we're ready to tackle the question that Mark raised earlier. How many Brands do we have?"

Chapter 31
Getting Focused

"Let's begin by discussing what you think is different about your Brand for your mid-price products," said Brandon as he once again stood before the whiteboard just behind the head of the table.

"Price, to state the obvious," said Mark. "But it's a bit more involved than just a number. We have to hit certain price points that our dealers demand and that our end-user customers require. We're dealing with an issue of affordability. We also have more competitors in the mid-price space than we have with our regular lines. We're being evaluated differently in the marketplace. It's more about price, functionality, and quality. Elegance and artistry are far down on the list of buying criteria. And for a significant segment of that market, all other things being relatively equal, price rules the day."

"And yet," said Joe, "some manufacturers in that market segment have begun to knock off some of our simpler designs. That tells me that a significant number of consumers in that demographic would like a more upscale, artistic look if they can get it at an affordable price. That was the main reason we acquired the companies we did."

"Joe, don't underestimate the importance of price in the middle market," Mark responded, "and don't ignore the prevailing, often irrational consumer mantra of wanting to have things 'faster, better, cheaper.' I'm as guilty as anyone, but I think that in our haste to acquire a presence in that market segment we may have ignored some strategic issues about the importance of price. One big challenge for us is this: For the companies who are trying to copy our designs, those Kitchen Sculpture knockoffs represent their product lines' high end. They have other products that perform most of the same functions but sell at lower prices. For us, our middle-market products are the lowest-price products we make. Not only that, but they generate the lowest gross profit margins of all our products. The result of all that is that customers who shop in those stores might be intrigued by our designs, but if they decide they want to spend less, we don't have anything to offer them—but our competitors do.

"So, given the disproportionate emphasis on price in the middle market, do we want our Brand potentially tarnished by price issues when we have such a strong image in our traditional, high-end market? And, if price alone becomes an overriding concern, aren't we better off with two Brands rather than one?"

"I hate to be the first one to say this. Wait; who am I kidding? I'm glad to be the first one to say this," said Desi, a tone of intensity in his voice. "Mark, with all due respect, you sound like a typical salesman. You just want to be able to sell at the lowest price to make your life easier. To me, that's bullshit."

"Of course you'd think that," Mark snapped. "You believe that your designs are priceless and that people should be willing to take out second mortgages to buy your blenders."

"Hold it; both of you," said Joe. "We're not even finished with our retreat, and you guys are back at it on a personal level. What the hell gives with you two?"

Desi and Mark stared hard at each other for several long seconds and, as if on cue, they both burst out laughing.

"I apologize," said Desi. "I started it."

"It didn't take much for me to get right into it," said Mark. "I'm sorry, too."

"I think we both just demonstrated that old habits die hard," said Desi, laughing. "Joe, thanks for jumping in. On the other hand, I was just getting warmed up. Another few minutes and we could've started charging admission and had every hotel guest in the building fighting to get in. Oh well."

When the laughter subsided, Brandon stepped in. "Sounds like we're starting to have that classic debate about price versus value."

"We are indeed," said Joe. "And contrary to what it sounds like, let me remind all of you—we've been down this road before. The context was different before. We were talking about marketing strategy. So I think it's good that we're revisiting the price-versus-value debate with the focus this time shifting to our Brand."

And so the discussion was unleashed. It raged up and down the emotional scale. But, as Brandon would later note, it stayed focused on the issues. It never got personal. Mark talked more about competing against both price and the wider variety of product choices offered by their competitors.

Desi countered with four strong arguments: (1) they were not going after the entire middle market, only the upper end of that category where *value* within the bounds of affordability, and not just the cheapest price, was the decision criterion; (2) the operating features and benefits they offered were still markedly superior to their competitors', at least for the present; (3) their reliability was the best in the industry, and because of that they could offer a ten-year warranty while the best their competitors offered was five years; and (4) Kitchen Sculpture's designs were far more elegant and carried the cache of their name to a portion of the middle market that valued their products' artistry, even though these consumers could not afford the price of their regular product line.

Manny and Ben initially opposed the suggestion of offering a ten-year warranty. But as they thought about it, they decided that their products really were reliable and sturdy enough to be able to offer the warranty without incurring excessive costs. And since their existing practice was to make and store spare parts for twenty-five years, it didn't seem to pose an additional, unreasonable inventory cost problem.

Ben was eager to run a series of sales volume iterations designed to show them what constituted acceptable sales, gross profit margin levels, and sales support costs to establish their performance goals; then, together with Mark's input, to assess the probabilities of achieving those goals.

Samantha contributed some innovative ideas regarding sales training for the personnel at their dealers' stores, using webinars, to increase the stores' reach and reduce their costs. She went on to discuss an array of internal training programs designed to fully integrate all their mid-price subsidiary companies' employees into the Kitchen Sculpture culture. There would no longer be two camps of "we/they"—there would be only one Kitchen Sculpture family.

Erika talked about the possibilities of using their mid-price products as a launching pad to develop their social media presence with both their dealers and end users.

Joe framed the discussion in terms of *both* executable strategies *and* the behaviors they would need to exhibit in order to firmly establish, in their customers' minds, the *what* and the *how* of their Brand.

The discussion was extensive, lively, engaging, and focused. It was simultaneously exhausting and energizing. Finally, Joe had heard what he needed to hear. "I think we've talked this through enough," he said. "And

I thank all of you for what I believe was one of the best discussions of this kind we've ever had."

All heads nodded.

"Here's what I think. Subject to Ben's projections supporting the direction and strategy that I'm about to propose, I believe we've landed on a decision. *We will have one Brand.* We'll develop a different family of names for our mid-price products. We'll further differentiate their identities with packaging and promotional messages. But the Kitchen Sculpture cache will be present in a way that appeals to the mid-price buyer without offending or confusing our high-end dealers and end-user customers."

It was a uniting moment, brought about not so much by Joe's decision, but by the process that spawned it. Everyone was stoked. It was the culminating climax that Joe had hoped for since this entire bizarre journey had begun.

Brandon quietly looked around at everyone in the room. He felt satisfied with what he saw. He smiled to himself. *Now,* he thought, *it's time to see if I can poke some holes in their happiness.*

Chapter 32

New Definition – New Culture

Brandon stood, walked to the head of the table, and surveyed the group. Their faces were engaged and eager; they were ready to start down their new path—ready to run a marathon at a sprinter's pace. *How naive they are,* he thought. *I think I could just sell them some mortgage-backed securities and get the hell out of here.... Stop it, Brandon. Get serious.*

"Folks," he began, "congratulations to all of you for the quality, mutual respect and the outcome of the process you just completed. You've worked hard, you've learned some valuable skills, you've applied those skills and have reached what you believe is the starting point of a new journey—one that will lead you to new heights in strengthening your Brand.

"Well, I don't want to discourage any of you, but I must point out that you have not reached the starting point."

Suddenly, puzzled looks from everyone replaced the excited ones of a minute ago.

"You heard me correctly," Brandon continued. "You have not reached the starting point. What you have done is arrived at a fork in the road, and it's a critically important fork, at that.

"You are at the juncture where we must now address the third question I wrote on the board a while ago: *Is it worth it?* At this moment, the answer is: *I don't yet know—and neither do any of you.* If you decide that it is worth it, you will take the fork we've been talking about this weekend. If you decide it's not worth it, you'll continue to treat your Brand the way you always have—the way most companies still do."

"Wait a minute," said Manny, somewhat perturbed. "We've invested a lot of valuable time and gone through some serious personal stuff. Why in the world—"

"Hold that thought, Manny," said Brandon. "I think I know where you're going, but let me continue, and I believe I'll address your concerns—perhaps all your concerns." Brandon shifted his gaze and made eye contact with everyone in the room as he spoke.

"You believe you have made a commitment to change, but your commitment is based on the emotion of the moment and does not yet embrace a full awareness of the harsh realities about what it takes to effect significant cultural change. My responsibility right now is to help you better understand the scope and depth of those realities.

"We need to do this for three reasons: first, it will better enable you to answer the question of whether or not it's worth it; second, it will help you understand the strength of commitment required from all of you to make this transition; and third, if you decide that what you're about to do is too much work, you'll have a full understanding of why you went back to accepting the traditional definition of what a Brand is. You'll also have a sense of why so many people and companies, even when they understand how consumers form opinions about a Brand and make decisions and recommendations based on those opinions, still choose to be delusional about how they define their Brands and how they spend their marketing dollars to support those delusions.

"When I speak of the emotion of the moment, what I'm really saying is that you have gotten a glimpse of *what is possible*. And I think we all agree that it is an exciting picture. So let's talk a bit about the journey—from your current reality to that future place.

"First of all, it doesn't occur overnight. It takes time. How much time? We don't know. And believe it or not, it doesn't actually matter. What matters is that there is a steady, noticeable, incremental shift. We're talking about cultural change: a shift in attitudes, beliefs, and behavior. With those kinds of changes come different results. But because the changes are usually small, they typically occur without drama. You have to look hard for reasons to celebrate; you must learn to recognize the importance of microscopic movement.

"A dealer who you have tried for years to break in with finally comes on board because he heard so many great comments about you from other dealers at an industry conference. Two dealers from different markets all of a sudden decide to broaden their line by adding your juice makers when they have never before sold juice makers. You suddenly receive a raft of comments, in e-mails and on your blog site, about the excellence of your customer service people, and those comments coincide with a slight increase in sales in the same geographic areas from where the comments came. A mid-price competitor of yours decides to discontinue their knockoffs of your products and goes back to their bread-and-butter, price-driven line because they can't compete with you on value for the money. Overall attendance at trade shows remains steady, but attendance at your booth increases by twenty percent over the previous year, and more dealers want your people to contact them. I think you get the picture.

"These kinds of changes come about because your Brand becomes stronger, not just bigger. They are the result of changes in your individual and collective behavior. *Effecting change of this type is a counter-intuitive process.*

In other words, many beliefs you hold, and habits you practice that you feel are right turn out to be wrong. And some that you feel are wrong turn out to be right. It's funny how that works. It's a process that puts you in a continual state of discomfort and resistance. Your challenge is to embrace the discomfort and overcome the resistance not by trying to avoid it, but by working through it. That takes patience, tenacity, and a strong commitment. It requires mutual support, coaching, and a willingness to look and feel awkward during your initial learning stages. Eventually new beliefs, new habits, and most importantly, new results replace old ones.

"Are you willing to incur the discomfort of ineptitude? Are you willing to feel lost and unsure for a time? Can you become and remain mutually supportive of one another? And if you do all of that, will the rewards justify your efforts? *Is all the change worth it?*"

Joe literally jumped to his feet. "I've been sitting here listening, just like all of you," he said. "And I can barely contain myself. Most important to me, and I hope to everyone else in the room, the answer is *yes, it's worth it!*

"Let me tell you why. Over the past two days, and especially while Brandon was speaking just now, I've been tossing around the questions in my mind: *What exactly is our Brand? What do we actually deliver as opposed to what should we deliver? What do we think is our Brand versus what our customers think?*

"I can't speak, at least not at this moment, for what our customers think. But I now have a clear picture in my mind as to what I want our Brand to be, and here it is. *To our end users—the ultimate consumers—we deliver great functional art, great value, and an unparalleled ownership experience. And to our dealers—our direct customers—we deliver great functional art, great value, and an unparalleled partnership experience.*

"I believe that everything we do to make a difference in the world will fit under that umbrella. I believe that our core values embrace that definition, and that the definition itself is consistent with our values.

"I also think that we already do many of the things needed to define us the way I just did. It's not as if we've been a complete bust at building our Brand; we're not starting from square one. We have a great reputation and a dominant position in our traditional, high-end market. We're the standard by which all others are judged.

"I think we all know that going into a market where there is intense competition among established players, and the retail price needs of the ultimate consumers and the wholesale price points demanded by the dealers are game changers that for us have presented challenges that we were too naive in assessing."

"And that could turn out to be a blessing in disguise," said Brandon, as he carefully surveyed each person in the room, studying their facial expressions and body language.

"You took the words out of my mouth," said Joe. "Look, people. I believe that the mid-price segment of the retail market might be the harbinger of the future for our entire business. I think it's dangerous for us to believe that we will *never* experience price competition in the high end of the market, or that no one will *ever* be able to compete with us in product design. So what better way for us to prepare for those new realities than by learning and adapting in the middle market, where at least price is already a factor? What more defining challenge can we overcome than taking the disparate cultures of our existing organization and those of our new, mid-price companies and blending them into a unified, compatible, highly productive whole? Do you all realize how strong that would make us?

"So as I said a minute ago, I can't tell you all how much I believe the answer to Brandon's third question—Is it worth it?—is a resounding *yes*. In fact, it's more than yes; it's not even an option—it's *crucial* to our success."

"I would like to add something to what's been so well said to this point," said Samantha as she stood, her posture and expression making her appear as if she were about to address an audience of a thousand shareholders.

The same thought hit Manny, Desi, and Erika simultaneously. *Just be yourself and drop the political posturing, girl. Oh well, you're a work in progress, just like the rest of us.*

Samantha continued. "I've seen these kinds of cultural change attempts before in my previous positions. And I agree with everything Brandon has told us. They're not easy. I've watched some attempts succeed, and I've watched others end up being abandoned, at great cost in both human and financial terms. And I can tell you that the difference between success and failure has been the quality of leadership and the strength of commitment and perseverance from the top, meaning all of us in this room. When we begin to put programs and procedures in place, a lot of people are going to balk and resist and rebel and offer reasons and excuses for not changing and tell us why certain things are bad ideas, and, and, and. If we allow that kind of behavior to overpower our commitment to change—then shame on us. We will have failed. Us—not them.

"For my part, from a training and coaching perspective, I intend to help create a culture where our Brand is continuously supported by people who have and exhibit the *right aptitudes, attitudes,* and *skills.* Now I know that right now, in this room, that sounds like a lot of rah, rah warm words, or as Manny might say—bullshit."

"Thanks for readin' my mind," Manny said with a big smile.

"And I know you all think I'm still a political animal," said Samantha. "And you're right. That has become part of my DNA. I'm working on exorcising it. But just because I still *sound* political, doesn't mean I *feel* political. Or that I'm *behaving* politically. Because I'm not. So I want you all to know that my mantra—for all the training and development work we do, and for our recruitment and hiring activities, and for the content of our performance reviews and the individual goal setting that emerges from that—my mantra is: I will work hard to make certain that we are constantly looking to improve our aptitudes, our attitudes, and our skills. I think that will help us achieve Brand strength. There, I've said my piece. Now, Ben, may I please have a blank check?"

"Sure," said Ben. "You know, all you have to do is ask," he smiled.

"But let me get serious for a moment...." Ben stood, as Samantha sat down. "I want to act in my usual capacity as devil's advocate. I've heard the same things as the rest of you, and I don't disagree with anything that anyone has said up to this point. My questions and my concerns are that I'm not hearing anything that's different or unique. I mean, this all sounds to me like basic textbook stuff. Management 101. I can see essentially this same discussion with the same answers happening in thousands or maybe tens of thousands of companies around the country. So what is going to make us stand out as being different or better?"

"Let me address that," said Brandon. "First of all, Ben, I think you make a good point; you've asked an important question and I'm glad you brought it up. There is only one thing: execution, brilliant execution," he said, his words hitting the group like sharp punches.

"Huh?" said Ben.

"The answer to your question as to what makes us different or better, is *brilliant execution*," Brandon repeated. "The power of your Brand lies in the brilliance of your execution. At the risk of being trite, and of offending anyone who isn't a sports fan, let me use a sports analogy, only because I think it will perfectly illustrate my point.

"Let's look at professional football, the NFL. All the teams in the league play the same game, with the same rules, same group of referees, same size field, same uniforms, same equipment, same complement of coaches, trainers, et cetera. They all play the game pretty much the same way. Every team's offenses run similar plays. Their defenses have similar formations and defend with similar patterns. Some play more zone, some more man-to-man, but they all get to choose from essentially the same options. OK. Let's look at the players. It's fair to say that every single player in the NFL is a gifted athlete. That's the ante to play at that level. If you're not gifted, you're not even going to get to put on a uniform. So they all have the *potential* to win. Yet every week, for the entire season, in every game, up to and including the Super Bowl, one team wins and one team loses. And what differentiates the winners from the losers? The quality and consistency of their execution. And brilliant execution (or its absence) involves much more than the raw skills of individual athletes. But starting with the athletes, there is the commitment to training and conditioning, the number of hours spent practicing, off-the-field strength training, cardio-vascular training, studying game films, learning the habits and tendencies of competitors, nutrition programs, off-the-field social activities. Some players see their God-given gifts as a ticket to a free ride, and some see them as a divine responsibility that they are honor-bound to fulfill. Then there is the quality, style, and commitment of coaches. The list goes on. But at the end of the day, when you put it all in a pot and stir it, you get the quality and consistency of execution. And the teams that do it best, week-in and week-out, usually come out on top. And the rest just play the game and struggle for survival.

"So Ben, and everyone else, that's where you are. You're correct when you talk about yourselves as being no different from thousands of other companies who have similar skills, issues, and opportunities. The question before you is, *What is the strength of your commitment to brilliant execution?"*

"Well," said Ben. "I've never played organized sports, much less at a professional level. But I can see what you are illustrating, Brandon. I can see it logically. I can begin to feel it emotionally. And it makes sense to me."

Heads around the room nodded. Some quiet time followed as everyone absorbed what had just been presented.

"Well then, Brandon," said Ben. "I have one last question. Since nothing you've talked about is top secret—in fact, it's fairly common knowledge at this point—why do only a minority of companies actually *do* what we're talking about? Why do most companies continue to define their Brands and strategize and spend their resources to support their Brands in the same old narrow way that we're about to change?"

"For the same reason that the vast majority of people don't eat healthy diets or exercise properly," said Brandon. "It requires more effort and discipline than they're willing to put forth. It's as simple as that.

"Most people are lazy. They're not necessarily physically lazy; they're mentally lazy. They're willing to work hard at what they already know, what they're already good at doing in their sleep, and what does not require them to experience the discomfort of change. They spend most of their time working hard and little to no time working smart. To work smart, one must embrace change. That involves facing fears, abandoning obsolete practices, and being uncomfortable in the process of learning new skills. The sad reality is that working hard but not smart only enables you to dig your own grave faster."

It was Desi's turn to speak. He appeared more serious and less dramatic than usual. "Let me add something that I think is important as well. I know that Joe has mentioned this a couple of times this weekend.

I'm talking about our silo mentality—the way all of us have maintained a guarded, proprietary attitude concerning our respective areas of responsibility. We've typically been unwilling to share information except on a self-determined, highly subjective 'need to know' basis. We've been unwilling to go the extra mile to help one another, to listen empathetically, and to understand our problems from a more global perspective. But we've been quick to point fingers when bad stuff happened. To me, it's felt like a kind of fear-stoked power play. And, now that I think about it, I also believe that some of us have been competing to be Joe's favorite.

"Well, people, from where I stand, if we continue to do that we have no chance of succeeding. We're doomed before we begin. Silos must end—and I mean today. From now on it's: *good-bye silos, hello collaboration."*

"Amen," said Joe.

"Amen," came the collective response.

"Well said," Brandon added. "Of course, just as it is with much of what we've talked about and you've decided, there's a gap between your intentions and your skills. But you can help each other a lot in this area. You can point out when silo-type behavior creeps back into someone's actions, and you can be receptive to hearing it when it applies to you. A new mantra that might work for all of you is: *Power comes from sharing."*

Brandon watched the group as a calm silence enveloped the room. Each person wore his and her own expression of contemplation. Finally, Joe spoke.

"Brandon," he said. "Where are we now?"

"Good question. Where do *you* think we are?"

"Personally, I think we have done what we came here to do," said Joe. "I feel complete, I feel that we've accomplished something important. And I'm feeling excited to begin this new chapter. How about the rest of you?"

"Me too," said Mark. "You've summed it up perfectly for me, Joe."

"Count me in," said Manny.

"I feel like we've just written the first draft of a Broadway play, and we're ready to begin rehearsals," said Desi, waving and gesturing to an imaginary theater audience. "Sorry, but it wouldn't be me without some drama thrown in."

"I'm good," Erika replied quickly in her usual deadpan.

"I'm feeling complete and excited," said Samantha.

"I can see tons of work ahead of us," said Ben, "and I'm good with all of it. I love where we're headed."

Brandon rose and walked to the head of the table. "Folks, we've done it. More precisely, you've done it. You've laid the groundwork to add depth and dimension to your Brand that can bring you to a new level of strength and ensure your continued growth and success for years to come. Executing won't be easy, but I believe you will find it immeasurably fulfilling. I'm so honored to have been part of your process. Joe, would you like to say a few words?"

Joe rose to speak as Brandon took his seat. "People, I'm proud of you. I'm proud of us. I applaud you not only for the content we developed, but also for the courage and honesty with which we created it. I could go on for hours, but I'll spare you and leave today with this: We have identified our challenges and our opportunities; we are clear as to how to address them. We know that brilliant execution is up to us. Our future is in our hands, and from where I sit, it's looking good. I love all of you. I'm proud and honored to lead you. Now go home and get some much-needed rest. The next step in our journey begins tomorrow."

Much sincere applause followed. Everyone hugged, shook hands, exchanged good wishes, and made their personal commitments to one another. When people looked around to thank Brandon, they noticed for the first time that he was gone.

What Next

Chapter 33

Debriefing–Sort Of

Joe's Monday morning began with an eerie sense of normalcy. No one who attended the retreat called or e-mailed him. And no word from Brandon. It was almost as if the retreat hadn't taken place. *Odd,* he thought. *Not at all like this group.* He attributed it to a combination of fatigue, information overload—they were still probably processing—and the usual heavy Monday workload. *Reactions will begin tomorrow.*

Joe's own day was filled with a heavy volume of calls to return, reports to review, and appointments to schedule for later in the week. He remained quite isolated and didn't see any of his executives during the morning.

He decided to have lunch sent in. Alice ordered him a sandwich, and he ate alone in his office while reading reports that recapped various meetings with customers and prospects from the mid-price division that Mark had forwarded to him.

His afternoon went by uneventfully as well—until three o'clock. Suddenly, he was struck by the same wave of fatigue that had hit him and heralded Brandon's otherworldly appearance about two weeks ago. *Had it really been just two weeks? It seemed like they had begun this endeavor months ago.*

He told Alice to hold his calls, walked over to his sofa, lay down, and was asleep before his head hit the cushions.

He first noticed that he felt cold. Then a pair of hands gently prodded his right shoulder. A voice penetrated the silence. "Mr. Fenington, wake up. Are you all right?" Alice stood over him as he regained consciousness. He noticed the concerned look on her face. *I just took a nap. Why the worried look?*

"Oh, boy," Joe muttered, sleep still clouding his voice. "I must have been really tired after all we've been through."

"Yes, sir, I know it was stressful on everyone," said Alice.

"Oh? Did you speak to any of the participants today?"

"No, Mr. Fenington, but I know how stressed you were this morning, and I know how late the meeting ended last night."

Joe looked at Alice with an expression of complete puzzlement.

She returned the look. "Mr. Fenington, are you feeling all right?"

"Yes, of course. Why do you ask? Alice, what time is it? How long have I been asleep?"

"It's almost six o'clock. You've been out for three hours."

"Wow, for someone who never takes naps that's a long time, especially when it happens twice in two weeks."

Alice turned pale. "Mr. Fenington, perhaps we should have you looked at by your doctor. I can get him on the phone right now."

"Alice, calm down. What in the world has you so upset? I just took a couple of naps, one after a stressful meeting and another one today, following our weekend retreat. I'm fine. I actually feel quite rested now."

Alice added a look of panic to her already ashen complexion. "What retreat?" was all she could say.

"Alice, let me ask you the same question. Are you OK?"

"No, Mr. Fenington, I'm not OK. I'm quite concerned about you."

"Why?"

"I'll tell you why. First, as you said before, you never take naps, but at three o'clock today you were overcome with exhaustion and took a three-hour nap. Then, when I woke you, the first thing you tell me is that you'd taken two naps."

"But … wait a minute, Alice. Today is Monday, right?"

"That's it. I'm calling your doctor. You just lie back down and I'll—"

"Stop," said Joe. "Just stop. Is today Monday or not?"

"Mr. Fenington, it's Tuesday evening and it's now around six fifteen. You've been soundly asleep for the last three hours. You had a stressful meeting with your management team last night over a product recall. You say you're rested and that you've taken not one but two naps over a two-week period. And you just asked me if today is Monday. I'm calling your doctor."

"Hold it," said Joe, anxiety now showing in his voice. "Alice, I need you to calm down and bear with me here. Let me get this straight. You're telling me that it's Tuesday evening and it's around six fifteen. It's not Monday. Is that right?"

"Yes sir, that's correct."

"And I laid down for a nap this afternoon—Tuesday—at three o'clock. And this is the first and only nap I've taken. Right?"

"Yes sir, right again. Now may I please—"

"No, Alice, you may not. Just stay with me. Now what I'm about to ask you is very important, so please pay close attention. Do you recall me introducing you to a man named Brandon Strong? He's a consultant working with us on our Brand. And did you set up some meetings with Mark, Manny, Desi, Ben, Erika, and Samantha? And did you arrange for a weekend retreat for the group at the Clearwater Springs Hotel? And did we hold that retreat this past Saturday and Sunday? And are you sure that today isn't Monday, and that I'm not losing my mind?" Joe was now rapidly pacing up and down the room, his face becoming redder and his voice more frantic with each step.

Alice's dumbstruck expression said it all. Joe walked unsteadily to his Eames chair and half sat, half collapsed into it. *What is happening? Is Alice right? Am I having some kind of attack? I don't know the symptoms, but is this the onset of a stroke? Maybe I should let Alice call my doctor. Wait. Calm down. Breathe. Let's just think for a minute.*

"Alice, let's both of us just sit still and think about what just happened." They both passed the next several minutes in silence, not daring to look at one another.

Finally, Joe broke the suspense with his laughter. "This cannot possibly be," he said. "There was too much clarity, too much detail. I remember every word, every emotion, every decision. Alice, I think I know what just happened."

"You do?" Alice hung on Joe's words like a drowning person to a lifeline, wanting him to make some sense of it all, needing him and the situation to normalize.

Joe continued to laugh, but now the tone of it became the laughter of relief. "Alice, everything I talked about, Brandon Strong, the meetings, the retreat, the day of the week—it was all a dream."

"It was?" Alice was still feeling a bit numb.

"Yes, it was. After our meeting last night, I was emotionally drained and physically exhausted. I must have fallen into a sleep so deep, and my dream was so intense and so vivid, that when I first awakened, I believed for a few minutes that it was all real, and the things I dreamed really happened. Alice, I'm sorry I scared you like that."

"So, you're really OK, Mr. Fenington? It was just a bad dream?" The color had come back to her face, and she appeared relaxed once again.

"Oh, it was a dream all right, Alice, but it wasn't a bad dream. It was a phenomenally good dream—one that I need to think about for a bit."

"Well, if you don't need me for anything, I've got some paperwork to finish up before I leave tonight. So I'll just go take care of that and leave you be."

"Fine," Joe replied, already lost in his thoughts. As he relaxed in his favorite chair, reflecting on the events of the past few moments, his mind began to pick up speed. *Could I have actually dreamed with that kind of clarity? I should write my memory of it all, before it disappears. This could be life-changing for the company. And Brandon Strong was just a figment of my imagination. But, man-oh-man, what an inspiring figment he was. What in the world made me conjure up a figure like that with a story like the one he told? I didn't take LSD, and I haven't eaten any strange mushrooms. Oh well, it is what it is. I'll start writing tonight. I need to chronicle my dream. We had some extraordinary breakthroughs, strengthened our team, improved our focus, charted the future for our Brand, and more. Wow. We dealt with all the issues that have been nagging at me and dragging me down for months. And now, I've got a handle on all of it. Amazing. I should take more naps.*

Joe rose from his chair and strode to his desk. Just as he was about to sit down, he noticed for the first time out of the corner of his eye a small, cream-colored envelope. It was perched in the middle of his meeting table. He could swear it wasn't there a few minutes ago.

He walked tentatively to the table, carefully sat down, and hesitantly picked up the envelope. It was expensive linen, of a size used for personal notes. Written across the face of the envelope, in large letters, was his first name—Joe. His hand trembled slightly as he opened the envelope and pulled out the handwritten note:

Joe,

You and your team did a great job during our time together. You made some profound decisions. As a result, you now have some wonderful opportunities, and you will face some significant challenges in the months ahead. I'm confident that you'll come out far better than I did.

I'll be around whenever you need me. I think you now know how to reach me.

All the best.

Brandon

The hair on the back of Joe's neck stood at attention. He stared in disbelief at the note in front of him. As he looked more closely, he noticed the uneven line widths of the pen strokes in the note. They immediately told him that it had been written with a fountain pen, the same kind of pen that he had referred to during the retreat. The hand holding the note began to shake when he tried to put it down.

I am going mad. I had a dream, but it wasn't a dream. And it wasn't real, either—at least it wasn't a reality that anyone besides me can see. I can't tell anyone. Who would believe me? What can I do?

Joe sat in silence for what seemed an eternity, but was, in reality, just five minutes. He had only questions, no answers. As he absentmindedly glanced around his office, his neck hair sprang back to attention. Brandon was sitting in his Eames chair, looking amused, relaxed, and smiling. Joe stifled a scream.

"What is happening to me?" Joe wailed, his voice suddenly frantic and quivering, beads of perspiration now dripping from his forehead. "A few minutes ago I thought I was going mad. As soon as I began to calm down, *you* materialize. Now I'm absolutely certain that I'm going bat-shit crazy. Alice was right. I need to have her get hold of my doctor."

"Relax, Joe," said Brandon, still smiling and relaxed. "Breathe deeply. Count slowly to ten."

"Go screw yourself—whoever, or whatever the hell you are." But despite his frantic defiance, he began to take deep breaths. His breathing slowed, his perspiration stopped, and his pulse rate dropped to nearly normal.

Brandon stared intently at Joe, patiently waiting for him to calm down enough to have a conversation. Several minutes of silence ensued. Finally, Brandon spoke. "Joe," he said, his speech slow and measured, "you're fine. You're not bat-shit crazy or any other kind of crazy. You had what you might describe as a dream, but it was more of a deep meditation.

You were in touch with your very core in a way that I suspect you have never before experienced."

"You can say that again," said Joe, speaking a bit more steadily. "And just where do you come in?"

"Think of me as your muse," said Brandon.

"My muse? Listen, Brandon, I'm no expert on muses, but you don't operate like any muse I've ever read about. And besides, muses used their inspirational powers in the creative arts like drama and poetry and dance."

"I admit I'm an unconventional muse. But, Joe, remember—you created me."

"Really? I created you? God, I hope this town has some good asylums, because that's where I'm about to take up residence."

"Joe, listen to me. This morning, you were exhausted. By mid-afternoon you had to take a nap. Issues had been building in the company and weighing on you for months. Soon after you fell asleep, you went into a meditative state. From that place, you explored the essence of your issues at a depth that enabled you to see and understand them in new ways. Your unconscious mind needed a guide—me—to lead you through this discovery process. Joe, this is your show. I'm just one actor."

"It sure as hell doesn't feel that way," Joe sounded lost. "I feel helpless, confused, out of control."

"That's because you've surrendered to a creative, introspective, spiritual process. The only way you can achieve that state is to let go, to give up your need to control."

"Control what?" asked Joe, sounding more confused.

"I'm talking about giving up your need to control your thoughts, the direction in which you're leading the company, intended outcomes, the birth of new ideas, new realities, new beliefs. You begin by suspending those needs and just listening. It's a path to real wisdom."

"I don't like it," said Joe. "I don't like not being in control. Frankly, it scares the hell out of me."

"Spoken like a true entrepreneur," said Brandon, with a wry smile. "But, Joe, think about this. You're engaged in a private process. You're only giving up control to another dimension of yourself. And you're only doing it for a brief period of time—in your case about three hours. No one else needs to know, unless you want to share. So what's the big deal?"

"Hmm, you might have a point there. I need to think about that."

"Joe." Brandon now sounded frustrated. "You went into a meditative state; you had an unbelievably great experience; you gained an enormous amount of knowledge and wisdom that you plan to bring to life in your company; and your future suddenly looks brighter than it has for some time. What the hell do you need to think about?"

"Well, for starters—*you*," Joe replied.

"What about me?"

"I'll tell you what. You present a great story about me creating you; about you being my muse, my guide, and whatever other bullshit you've come up with along the way. But the bottom line is this: I'm sitting here, talking to myself. You're telling me that I'm in touch with my inner self. But the rational part of me has another word for it—*schizophrenia*."

By the time Brandon stopped laughing, a stream of tears was running down his cheeks. He finally collected himself. "Joe," he said, still trying to erase his smile, "when you were a little boy, did you ever have any imaginary friends? They could have been people of any age, animals, fictional characters, or perhaps people that were your heroes at the time. Anyone at all?"

Joe thought for several moments. "As a matter of fact, I did," he said with a surprised look on his face. "I did. My friends were the cowboy heroes of the day from TV and the movies. I remember they would come to our apartment, usually around lunchtime, sit at the table, and eat with me. We'd have conversations—out loud. When my mother tried to sit down to eat, I would tell her that she couldn't sit in a particular chair because my *friend* was sitting there. I think I had three or four *friends* but only one at a time would show up for lunch."

"What happened to your *friends?*" Brandon asked.

"I grew up. They were make-believe, childish fantasies. Lots of kids have them, including my own, when they were little. It was cute, up to a certain age."

"Did your mother think you were schizophrenic? Did you think your kids were schizophrenic?"

"No, of course not. What are you getting at?" Joe's impatience was obvious.

"What you were experiencing as a child was a journey of creativity; you were using your imagination," Brandon said, his expression and tone deadly serious. "And what your mother did, and probably what you did, and definitely what our society does is to teach our kids that creativity has no place in the *normal* part of our lives. *And that, my friend, is the real bullshit we're talking about.*

"Joe, you haven't engaged your creative mind or been truly introspective for so long that that part of you has atrophied. You solve problems, you analyze opportunities, and you envision your future using only your *rational* mind and linear logic. You were pushed to the brink by the pressures of the day, and you finally connected with your inner core, and now you're so frightened by the quality of the outcome that you are questioning your sanity.

"You and your entire culture, with the exception of Desi and the creative team, have come to define creativity as resourcefulness and adaptability. Those things don't represent true creativity. All I can say is, thank God you have Desi. And by the way, how do you and your team react to Desi when he is expressing his creativity? *Like he's nuts, that's how*. You tolerate his *eccentricity*, until you can transform his *ideas* into something *practical*. Sure, you respect his genius; you're just too inhibited to want to *engage* in his process. Shame on you."

"You know, Brandon, there are such things as sales, profitability, positive cash flow, and having a strong balance sheet to consider. Those little, insignificant things."

"Oh, stop it," said Brandon, obviously annoyed. "You're never going to lose sight of economic viability. That's a given. Everyone, even Desi, knows that. So don't use the need to achieve measurable results as an excuse to avoid looking deeply inside yourself, or not to engage your imagination.

"Joe, *not all challenges are best solved by running faster*. Look at what just happened: you stopped running; you looked deeply and profoundly inside yourself; and you invented me to help guide you. You did what I call *speeding up by slowing down*. You can call it crazy if you like. I call it *brilliance*. And we know that there is always a fine line separating the two.

"Think of it this way. You were offered a gift, the gift of insight. You accepted it. You embraced it. You are now poised to experience its benefits."

"But why me? What makes me so special?" Joe asked, aiming a pensive stare at Brandon.

"Joe, everyone is special. But few people see themselves in that light. Most people just go about their lives in a kind of survival stupor. And being special is not about having enough money and enough of the stuff that money can buy. I'm talking about being *relevant*. Very few people ever question their relevance in the game of life. Are they doing what they were put on earth to do, and feeling passionate about whatever that happens to be? Do they even know what that something is? Are they making a difference?

"Joe, everyone has the opportunity to be relevant. And becoming and remaining relevant is the closest thing to finding the fountain of youth that anyone will ever experience in this life. It requires being on a continuous journey of learning and self-discovery. What you've just done is a perfect example of that. We can't achieve eternal youth in the physical sense, but we can remain young for more of the years that we're physically present simply by remaining relevant, because relevance is energizing. That's what you were doing when you took your little journey. Be proud of yourself, Joe. Be grateful. You started something good."

"Brandon, I just wanted a stronger Brand. And I didn't even know I needed *that*, until you showed up—or, if I believe you, until I invented you. You're making it sound like I'm suddenly some great spiritual leader—the next Dalai Lama maybe."

"Joe, what I'm trying to tell you is that you're on the right path. If it sounds grand to you, it's because doing it this way is new to you and right now, it seems overpowering. But, Joe, it's a prescription for growth that anyone who wants it can have.

"We worked to strengthen Kitchen Sculpture's Brand. But Kitchen Sculpture is itself just a metaphor for every company out there. And some have already embraced and put into practice all the things we've *discovered.*

"Perhaps even more importantly, Kitchen Sculpture is a metaphor for every *individual,* every single *person* out there. We've said it before, but it's such a strong truth. All of us have our own Brand, based on the *what* and the *how* of our presentation to the world of who we are. And, of course, just as it is for Kitchen Sculpture, it's based on our actions, not our words."

Joe sat silently, contemplating, sifting and sorting, trying to get his head around what he was experiencing, what he had just heard. Had he really just conducted a conversation with himself—at a depth that revealed an unconscious wisdom that he hadn't known existed? If that was true, was it also true that everyone has the power to do that if they really want to?

He looked over at Brandon, sitting in his Eames chair, looking perfectly content, satisfied, relaxed. "I'm trying to grasp what has happened, what is still unfolding," said Joe. "I still have so many questions."

"For example?" Brandon asked.

"For starters," said Joe, "how about that whole over-the-top story of the Brand revolution, and you dropping dead from a heart attack, and God giving you this assignment, and…the rest of that other-worldly fable?"

"Simple," Brandon shot back. "Your conscious resistance to the process was so strong that only a truly bizarre story would allow the door to your unconscious mind to open. So you created that story. What else?"

"OK," said Joe, "how is it that you said many things that never would have come out of my mouth? The new definition of our Brand, for example. Explain that."

"That's easy," Brandon shot back. "That was just you giving yourself permission to think, conceptualize, and speak outside the prison of your current beliefs. You freed yourself from the shackles of your intellectual inhibitions. As to defining your Brand, you had been searching for a better definition for some time. You felt it, but you had to go deep inside yourself to find the words. You created me to help you get there. Next?"

"How about the note you wrote to me," said Joe. "With a fountain pen, no less. How do you explain that? How do *I* explain that? That's physical evidence that *I* did not invent you."

"What note?" asked Brandon. "There is no physical note. Joe, you created that note in your mind. Your unconscious mind acknowledged the good work you did. It told you that I'm here for you whenever you need me. And it reassured you that you know how to reach me."

Joe's eyes darted to his table. The top was clean. He looked at the floor around the table. There was no note. "Brandon, this is nuts," he said, looking back to the chair where Brandon sat.

Brandon was gone.

Joe stared at the empty Eames chair as he slowly rose from his seat, then methodically paced back and forth across his office. He looked straight ahead, blankly, as if waiting for some sign to emerge, like a giant billboard on an unlit road in the middle of the night with a brightly lit message flashing all the answers to all his questions. There was no billboard. And there were no answers, at least not yet.

But after a time, there did emerge a sense of direction, a way to begin, and a path to follow while he explored the possibilities of his experience and searched for his truth.

He went to his phone and buzzed Alice. She was still at her desk. He asked her to come in.

"Alice, I know it's late, but I want to give you an important project to get started on first thing tomorrow morning."

"Of course, Mr. Fenington."

"I want you to set up a series of one-on-one meetings for me with all of our senior vice presidents as soon as possible. Each meeting will be held in their respective offices and each one should last for about an hour. Then I want you to contact the folks at the Clearwater Creek Hotel and get some available weekend dates for a two-day retreat for our group about two weeks from now. Got it?"

"Yes, sir. Got it."

"Any questions?"

"Yes, Mr. Fenington. What should I tell everyone these meetings are about? You usually like to give people an agenda in advance so they can be prepared."

"Tell them it's about our Brand, Alice. Yes, tell them it's about our Brand."

Epilogue
It Needn't End Here

Your encounter with a new definition of your Brand should not end here. I've created a place where you can continue to learn, to explore and to gather new ideas and wisdom.

Go to: www.billleider.com. Visit frequently. It's a website whose sole purpose is to expand on the practical applications of Brand presented in this book. By going to the website, you'll have the opportunity to read a continuing series of blog posts about Brand, hear what others have to say, what they have seen and continue to experience by applying this definition to their organizations and to their personal lives. From time to time you'll get to read some real-life stories of people and companies that have gotten it right with respect to truly understanding what their Brand means and have built their entire culture around it. Of course, you'll get to join the conversation, offer up your own opinions and your stories so that you can help make a difference in the lives of others.

Your journey has just begun. Join the movement. Enrich your life. Check out www.billleider.com. It's just a click away.

Acknowledgments

I'm a late bloomer and this is my first book. I think, in a way, that's a blessing for my readers and for me. It allowed me more years to have the experiences that found their way into this book, to meet and work with so many people — clients and colleagues — whose views and skills and personalities helped shape my own perspective. I believe that made for an experientially richer, more relevant and more valuable book. So I want to first, thank all of them for helping me become aware of and honor our differences and for being the foundation of the characters and interactions in this story.

Thanks to Amy Friedman, one of my writing teachers at UCLA, for her skill as a teacher, her patience and encouragement along the way, and to Elaine Partnow for her firm but gentle touch as my editor.

To Eric Openshaw, my long-time client, colleague and most importantly my close, close friend whose critical observations and suggestions were instrumental in bringing to print some important messages. Without him, this book would have been severely lacking.

To Jeff Turner, client, partner, colleague and friend. Thank you for your stirring introduction and for helping to keep the characters honest and complete throughout my writing journey.

To my two phenomenal daughters, Janet and Heather, who endured endless hours of conversation, multiple readings of the same stuff, their valuable input that polished the nuances and made the dialogue more authentic. And for their constant support and encouragement every step along the way.

And finally to my beautiful, supportive, patient, inspirational, loving wife, Arlene. Her constant encouragement and praise gave me so much positive energy. I cannot imagine how I could have written this book without her. Thank you sweetheart. I love you.

About the Author

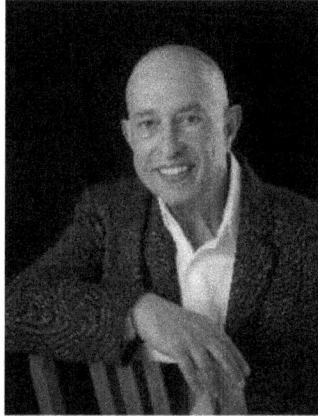

Bill Leider has worked for over thirty-five years as a strategic consultant to organizations – from Fortune 500's to entrepreneurial startups, and everything in between. His experience has embraced dozens of industries. In the course of his work he has helped companies define and hone their brands as an integral part of the entire organization's focus, and has assisted in implementing the cultural shifts needed to transform organizations. Along the way, he has also served as the CEO of several companies, both publicly traded and privately owned. It is through that body of work that he developed and honed his holistic views of what a brand truly is, how organizations can benefit by adopting that concept, and how to formulate and execute practical strategies and shape cultures to make those benefits a reality.

www.billleider.com

www.ingramcontent.com/pod-product-compliance
Lightning Source LLC
Chambersburg PA
CBHW070551200326
41519CB00012B/2186